Content

Instructions

Your brain is the most powerful machine in the known universe.

It is capable of amazing feats of deduction and of incredible leaps of creativity – if only you'll let it!

Most of us take our brains for granted. Unlike the external parts of our body, we can't see what's going on inside our heads, so we tend to just assume that it's all okay and get on with the rest of our lives.

Well, it turns out that it's absolutely worth investing some time in caring for your brain. The fact is, it's your brain that makes you *you*. Without it, you wouldn't be able to do anything. You also wouldn't know who you were, what you were, where you were – or have a clue what to do next, or even what you'd just finished doing. So your brain is critical to every aspect of your existence, and it's well worth taking the time to look after it.

Looking after your brain
So what can you do to care for your brain?

Just as your body needs physical exercise, so your brain needs mental exercise. You should aim to challenge yourself as often as possible – and certainly every day – with a range of tasks.

If parts of your day-to-day routine have become mundane, change them. Take a different route to work, have something unusual to eat for dinner, or travel to somewhere you haven't been before.

Try a new hobby – or several hobbies – and learn a new language. Take up a musical instrument, or another one if you already play. Read books on topics that you wouldn't normally consider, or try watching documentaries on subjects you know nothing about.

Whatever it is you decide to do, the most important thing is that you give your brain lots of new experiences. Your brain loves to learn, and it can learn the most from something it hasn't encountered before.

BOOST YOUR BRAIN

PUZZLES TO IMPROVE YOUR MENTAL FITNESS

ARCTURUS

ARCTURUS

This edition published in 2019 by Arcturus Publishing Limited
26/27 Bickels Yard, 151–153 Bermondsey Street,
London SE1 3HA

ISBN: 978-1-78888-682-6
AD006846NT

Printed in China

Instructions (continued)

How to use this book

This book won't teach you a new language or instrument, or help you travel, but what it *can* do is provide as wide a range of fresh mental challenges as it's possible to include in a single book!

It's packed full from front to back with a huge range of different puzzles, including many that you are unlikely to have encountered before. Remember that you need to challenge your brain, so don't skip over the puzzles that you find tricky or confusing – the chances are, these are the ones that will provide the greatest mental gains.

Each puzzle includes a difficulty star rating, given at the top of the page, rated from one up to three stars. More stars means trickier, but how difficult you find a puzzle will depend on your existing experience, so they are intended to be used only as a guide.

You can dip into the book as you please, but you'll get the greatest benefit if you start at the beginning and work your way through in order. There are a few reasons for this:

» The book includes hints and tips information every few pages, and these will make most sense if read through in order. Some of the information, and the tips themselves, are cumulative in nature – so they will make more sense when read in the order in which they are presented.

» The puzzles in the book do generally get progressively trickier and more complex as you progress, as indicated by the star ratings, so if you jump in at the end you might be in for a bit of a shock!

So, once you're ready, let's turn the page and get started!

Hints and Tips

A Healthy Body and a Healthy Mind

» We're often told about the importance of looking after our bodies, so that we can maintain our physical fitness and improve our chances of staying healthy. But it's all too easy to neglect looking after our brains, despite the fact that they are central to everything we are. Every thought, every deliberate movement and every memory is contained within our brains.

» Looking after your brain certainly does involve ensuring suitable mental exercise, but it's important not to forget that your brain, just like your other organs, is powered by the rest of your body. So while it may seem that physical fitness and intelligence are unrelated, they are in fact linked. This means, therefore, that looking after your body is important for your mental health.

» Each of your brain cells has a limited amount of energy, which is quickly used up and so needs to be replenished – and the fitter you are, the more quickly this can happen. It's also important to have a healthy, balanced diet, so that your brain has access to all the chemicals it needs to function.

» It is important for your brain health that you find time to move and stay as healthy as you can – which can be no easy feat with the many requirements we all have on our time. Try to build physical exercise into even static routines, such as sitting at a desk – for example, by getting up for a regular brief walk. Even small movements or standing every so often can help to improve circulation, which is beneficial for your brain.

» There is no one-size-fits-all for fitness – so aim to find a physical activity that suits you. If you don't like gyms or running tracks, try something with less impact such as yoga or Pilates. Try cycling or walking to destinations, if it is safe to do so, instead of using more passive means of transport.

Futoshiki

Place a digit from 1 to 7 into each empty square, so that each digit appears once in every row and column. You must place the numbers so they obey the inequality signs between some squares. The arrow always points to the smaller of the two numbers.

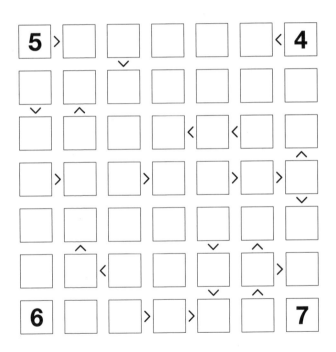

Binary Numbers

Write either a 0 or a 1 into each empty square, so that each row and each column contains five 0s and five 1s.

The numbers must be written so that no more than two of any number occur immediately next to one another within any row or column. For example, "01001101" would be fine, but "01000110" would not, due to the three 0s in immediate succession.

					1			1	1
0					1			0	1
			1					1	
		1		1	1				1
0	0				0			0	
						0	0		
1	1			0	0				
			1	0		1			
		0						0	0
	1					0			

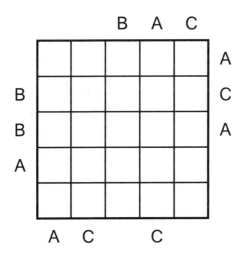

3

Easy as A, B, C

Place the letters A, B and C once each into every row and column of the grid. This means that two squares in each row and column will remain empty.

Letters given outside the grid reveal the letter that is encountered first when reading along that row or column from the given letter.

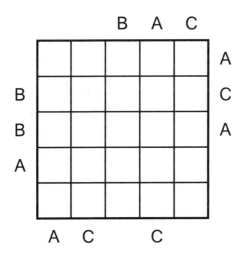

Number Wall

Test your number skills by writing a number from 0 to 9 into every empty square of this numerical wall.

Numbers must be placed so that each column of white squares adds up to the value given in the bottom, shaded square of that column. For example, the five white squares in the first column must sum to a total of 17.

Identical numbers cannot touch – not even diagonally.

Finally, a number cannot repeat within a single row. This means that every row must contain each number from 0 to 9 exactly once each. Note that numbers *can* repeat within a column, subject to the no-touching rule.

1						5		7	
				1					
5	0	6	3	4		8			
	8	4		6	0			5	
0	7	3		5		8	6	9	
17	27	23	19	21	20	29	22	30	17

5

Fences

Can you complete this fence, by connecting exactly two fence panels to each fence post? Fences are represented by either horizontal or vertical lines, and some are drawn in already.

The finished fence must form a single loop that visits every post once.

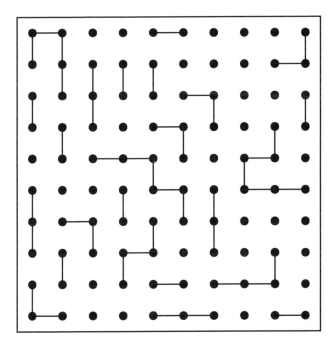

Quad Fit

Place a digit from 1 to 7 into every square so that each digit appears once in every row and column.

Groups of four digits are placed on the intersection of some sets of four squares. These four digits must be placed, once each, into the four squares that surround the group. They are sorted into numerical order, so it is up to you to work out which square each one must go in.

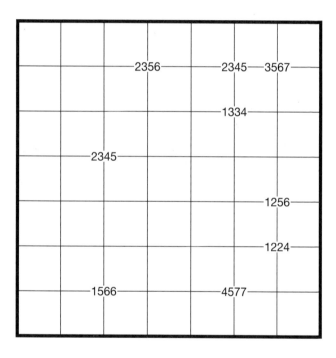

Meadows

New experiences can include all kinds of challenges for your brain, so why not start with this unusual puzzle type featured below?

Draw along the dashed grid lines to divide this "meadow" up into a number of squares, of size 1x1 or larger, so that every region formed in the grid is a perfect square – and there are no grid squares left over that are not part of any shape. Also, each of those regions must contain exactly one "cow", represented by the circles.

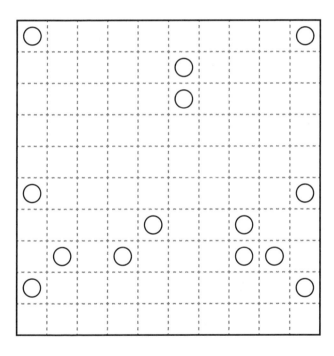

Spiral Galaxies

In this unusual puzzle, the aim is to draw along the grid lines to form a rotationally symmetrical shape around each of the circular "pivots" marked in the puzzle. Two shapes are marked in already to show you how the pivots work. Notice how these shapes could be rotated 180 degrees around their pivots and yet still look identical.

The shapes must be placed so that every square in the grid is part of exactly one shape. This means that shapes cannot overlap.

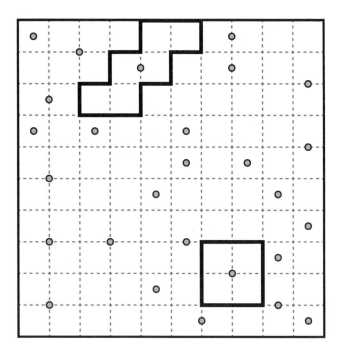

Brain Chains

Mental arithmetic skills are incredibly important in everyday life, whether you're making sure you aren't being overcharged when shopping, or working out what to pay when you have to split a restaurant bill. For practice, try solving all of these brain chain puzzles without making any written notes – that is, just in your head. For each chain, follow every step in turn from the given number until you reach the final result. Write this number in the box at the end of the chain.

| 13 | ×4 | +21 | -15 | ×1/2 | -21 | RESULT |

| 9 | ×8 | +1 | -32 | +16 | -27 | RESULT |

| 17 | +1 | ×1/2 | √ | ×8 | +50% | RESULT |

| 38 | ×1/2 | +71 | -72 | ×3 | -48 | RESULT |

| 57 | ×1/3 | ×8 | -81 | +72 | ×10/13 | RESULT |

Nurikabe

Shade some of the empty squares so that each number remains in an unshaded region of the given number of squares. There must be exactly one number in each unshaded region in the completed puzzle.

Shaded squares cannot form any 2×2 (or larger) areas, and all shaded squares must also form a single continuous region.

Regions count as continuous if squares touch to the left, right, above or below – but not diagonally.

2						5			
		2							
			3		2		2		2
2									
	1			3			3		
								3	
		4		2					
3						2			4

Link Words

Each of the following pairs of words secretly conceals a third word. This third word can be added to the end of the first word, and the start of the second word, to form two new words.

Can you reveal all six hidden words? For example, GRID _____ SMITH would be hiding the word LOCK, to make GRIDLOCK and LOCKSMITH.

SAND _ _ _ _ _ WORK

REGRET _ _ _ _ _ SPOON

OVER _ _ _ _ _ ION

HEAD _ _ _ _ _ TICS

FINGER _ _ _ TOE

Hints and Tips

Train Your Brain

» Your brain is incredibly complex. It must be, to be able to encompass all of the incredible variety of human thought that exists, let alone the complex thoughts, dreams and memories of any single individual. Therefore, despite many scientific advancements, much of it remains something of a mystery.

» What we do know is that you can strengthen and protect your cognitive abilities through learning. This idea is encapsulated by the term "brain training", which in turn covers two main concepts. Firstly, that if you don't make use of your abilities, you will lose them – which has essentially proven to be true. And, secondly, that by exercising one skill you can become significantly better at some other, seemingly unrelated skill – so-called "far transfer".

» Unfortunately, if the "far transfer" effect exists, no one really knows for sure how to trigger it, so your best bet for brain training is to simply try as many varied, challenging activities as you can. Once a particular activity becomes routine, you are probably gaining significantly less mental benefit from it. As a result of this, there are many different puzzles in this book, and each individual puzzle type appears no more than a few times.

» A corollary of the difficulty of finding activities that lead to "far transfer" is that you should make an effort to move outside your mental comfort zones. Don't just stick to activities that you're familiar with, but instead experiment with new experiences. No matter how old you are, it's never too late to try something new, and generally your own inhibitions are all that hold you back. So remember that you owe it to yourself to look after your brain, and you should give as many new things as you can a try.

» One place to start is with the wide range of activities in this book. Given the diverse skills required to tackle them all, this book should make a great beginning on your brain-training journey.

Loop Finder

You can begin training your brain with this loop puzzle, where the aim is simply to draw a single loop that visits *every* white square. The loop can travel only horizontally or vertically between touching white squares, and cannot cross over itself or enter any square more than once.

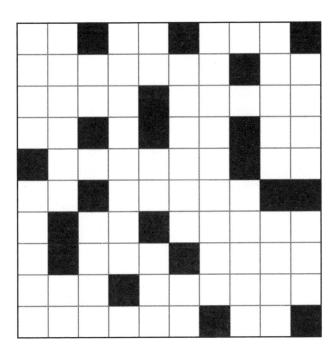

Circular Pairs

Draw straight horizontal or vertical lines to join each white circle to exactly one shaded circle.

Lines cannot cross over either another line or over a circle.

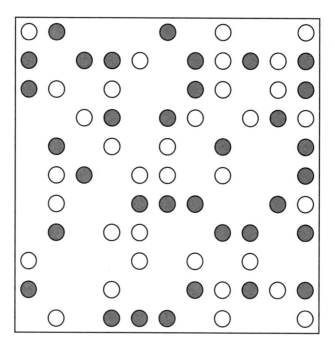

Word Pyramid

Can you complete this word pyramid by solving the clues, placing one letter per square? Each row will contain the exact same letters as the previous row, plus the addition of one extra letter – although the order of the letters may be rearranged.

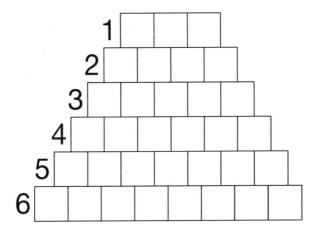

1. Canine

2. Precious metal

3. Rustic accommodation

4. Yearned

5. Sat around idly

6. Hit with a club

Ripple Effect

Place a digit into each empty square so that every bold-lined region contains each digit from 1 up to and including the number of squares in that region. For example, a 4-square region must contain the digits 1, 2, 3 and 4.

Also, no digit can be placed so that it is within that many squares of an identical digit in either a horizontal or vertical direction. This means, for a digit *x*, that there must be at least *x* squares (which do not contain the digit *x*) between that digit and any other occurrence of that digit in the same row or column.

1			1	4	3	1	
		4		1			3
3			5			3	
1	4		1	3			1
			2	1	3	5	
4		3					1
	2	1	3	2			3
2		5			2	3	

Number Link

Draw ten paths in the grid, each joining a pair of identical numbers. The lines must pass horizontally or vertically between the middles of touching squares, and cannot cross or touch at any point.

1								
2				2			3	
	4	5			5			
				6	4	7	3	
1		8			7	9		
			9					10
6								
8		10						

Killer Sudoku

Place a digit from 1 to 9 into every square so that each digit appears once in every row, column and bold-lined 3×3 box.

Digits in each dashed-line cage must add together to give the total printed at the top-left of that dashed-line cage. Digits cannot be repeated within any individual dashed-line cage.

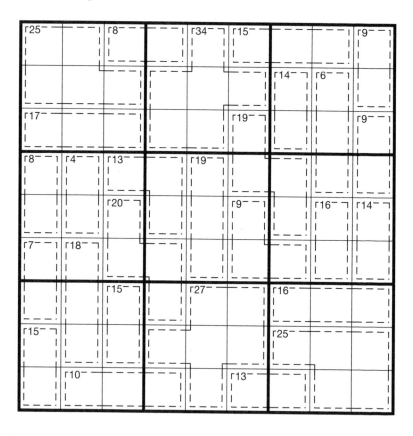

Sudoku

Place a digit from 1 to 9 into every empty square so that each digit appears once in every row, column and bold-lined 3×3 box.

	2			7			4	
4	1						9	7
			1		3			
		8	6		1	9		
9								5
		5	4		2	1		
			7		5			
3	5						6	2
	8			2			5	

Sets

Draw along some of the dashed lines to divide the grid up into 12 separate regions, each containing the letters A to F exactly once.

D	A	E	F	B	E	F	A
F	D	E	E	A	C	B	C
A	C	F	B	D	D	D	A
C	E	C	B	A	B	F	E
A	B	E	B	C	E	C	C
D	E	F	A	F	F	D	D
F	D	B	C	A	B	E	D
C	A	D	F	A	D	C	B
E	B	B	C	F	E	A	F

Wordoku

Place a letter in each square so that there are nine different letters in the grid, and no letter repeats in any row, column or bold-lined 3×3 box.

When you are finished, a word will be spelled along the shaded diagonal.

	F			N	W		R	
E		W						
R				S				
	L	O			S	N		
		S				R		
		U	W			F	L	
				U				F
						O		L
	W		L	F			S	

Number Pyramid

Write a number in each empty block in this pyramid. The numbers must be chosen so that every block contains a value equal to the sum of the two blocks immediately beneath it.

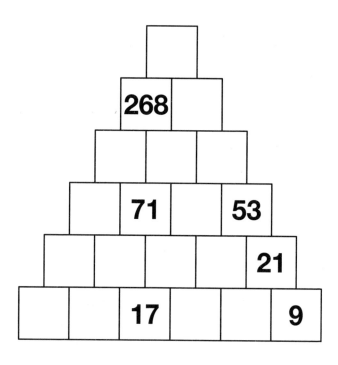

Futoshiki

Place a digit from 1 to 7 into each empty square, so that each digit appears once in every row and column. You must place the numbers so they obey the inequality signs between some squares. The arrow always points to the smaller of the two numbers.

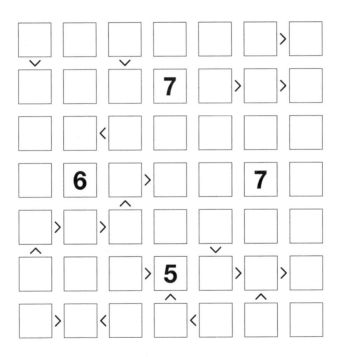

Hints and Tips

Thinking Logically

» The puzzles in this book are designed to make you think, so that you give your brain a good exercise. Many of them involve thinking logically to solve a puzzle, which may in itself be a skill that you might feel you lack. But the truth is, thinking logically doesn't require any special talent, over and above the innate skill to reason that we are all born with.

» Thinking logically is simply a process of recognizing what you're looking at, thinking about what it involves and then taking the time to start to explore the implications of those thoughts. Logical thinking encompasses finding connections and then deducing information from those connections. In the case of the puzzles in this book, it means working out what first and subsequent steps you can deduce from the information you are given.

» Logical reasoning is essentially a series of "what if" questions. If you take this step, how will it affect everything else? With regards to logic puzzles, the "what if" questions are especially significant because the puzzles are designed so that you can make successive deductions through observation. Therefore, logic puzzles are a fantastic way to exercise logical thinking.

» In general, it is wise to spend some time thinking about the real meaning of information. For example, when you read an article about research that has been done concerning a specific topic, try to think about it logically before blithely accepting the results. How was the data gathered? Is the number of participants in a medical study really that meaningful? In other words, try to make an effort to engage in logical and critical thinking when processing new information.

» If you are unsure how to begin a logic puzzle, try an exploratory trial-and-error method (i.e. guess!). It's amazing what you can learn from experimenting, and you can always erase your initial guess if it turns out to be wrong.

Shaded Rooms

Shade some of the grid squares in such a way that no two shaded squares touch one another – except diagonally – and so that all unshaded squares form a single continuous area.

Numbered squares may or may not be shaded, but always give the exact amount of shaded squares in a bold-lined room.

Any continuous horizontal or vertical run of unshaded squares cannot cross more than one bold line.

1				0		2			
0									
				3		1			
						2			
								3	
	2								
1	0	4					0		
		1			2				

Light Up

Draw light bulbs in some of the squares so that every white square is lit. Light bulbs illuminate all squares in the same row or column until the first black square they encounter – i.e. light does not pass through the black squares. Light bulbs cannot illuminate one another, although more than one light bulb may illuminate an empty square.

Squares with numbers must contain that many light bulbs in the adjacent squares (i.e. squares touching to the left, right, above or below). Not all light bulbs are necessarily indicated by number clues, however.

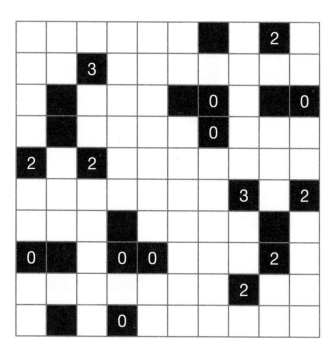

Line Sweeper

Draw a loop that passes through the middle of some squares, using only horizontal and vertical lines. The loop can enter each square only once, and so cannot touch or cross over itself at any point.

Numbers in the grid reveal the number of touching squares that the loop enters, including diagonally touching squares.

2							2
		7	6				
				7			
						7	
	8						
				6		5	
						6	
		5					

Lighthouses

Place ships in some of the grid squares, so that every ship is lit by at least one lighthouse. Lighthouses are the numbered, black squares. Lighthouses illuminate all squares in the same row or column, irrespective of whether another ship or lighthouse is in the way.

Each lighthouse must light up the given number of ships. Also, ships cannot touch either each other or a lighthouse – not even diagonally.

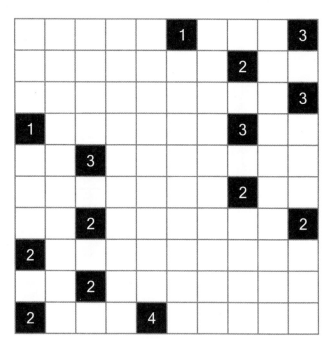

Walls

Draw either a horizontal or a vertical line in each empty square, so that each line passes through the middle of the square and runs the full width or height of the square. In this way, runs of horizontal lines in horizontally adjacent squares form a single longer line that passes through multiple squares, and similarly for vertical lines in vertically adjacent squares.

Numbered squares in the grid reveal the total length of all the lines that touch those squares, measured in terms of the number of grid squares the line passes through.

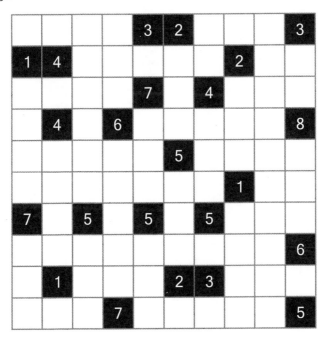

Samurai Sudoku

Place a digit from 1 to 6 into every empty square so that each digit appears once in every row, column and bold-lined 2×3 box of the three overlapping 6×6 sudoku grids. The grids must be solved together in order to reach a unique solution.

LITS

Shade some squares to create one tetromino within each bold-lined area. A tetromino is a shape made up of four adjacently touching squares. Tetrominoes must be L, I, T or S shapes, but not a solid 2×2 box, so these are the four options:

All shaded squares in the puzzle must form a single connected area, as in the example solution to the right. Conversely, there must not be any shaded areas of 2×2 squares (or larger).

No two of the same type of tetromino (L, I, T or S) may touch, except diagonally. Reflections and rotations of the same type of tetromino still count as the same tetromino, and therefore may not touch one another.

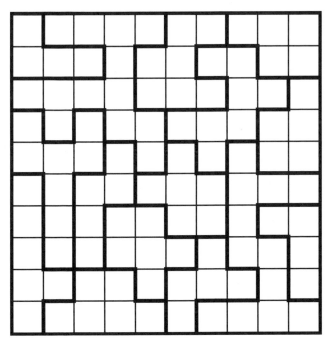

Bridges

Draw horizontal and vertical lines to join pairs of numbers, so that all the numbers connect together to form one large connected set. This means that you can start on any number and follow lines to reach any other number.

Lines cannot cross over either another line or over a number, and each number must have the exact number of connecting lines given.

There can be no more than two lines joining any given pair of numbers.

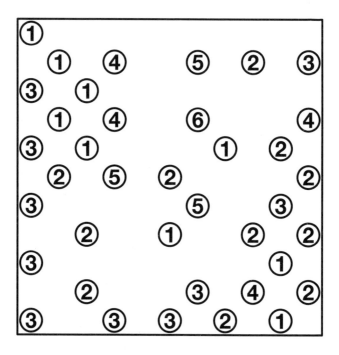

Calcudoku

Place a number from 1 to 6 in each square so that each number appears once in every row and column. Also, the numbers in each bold-lined region must result in the number given at the top-left when the given operation is applied between all the numbers in that region. For subtraction and division, start with the highest number in the region and then subtract or divide by the remaining numbers.

4÷	4−		40×	90×	
	5−				
12+	7+			0−	
		40×	2÷		
90×			6÷		3÷
			3−		

Number Wall

Test your number skills by writing a number from 0 to 9 into every empty square of this numerical wall.

Numbers must be placed so that each column of white squares adds up to the value given in the bottom, shaded square of that column. For example, the five white squares in the first column must sum to a total of 14.

Identical numbers cannot touch – not even diagonally.

Finally, a number cannot repeat within a single row. This means that every row must contain each number from 0 to 9 exactly once each. Note that numbers *can* repeat within a column, subject to the no-touching rule.

		5	8						
0			7	2	4	6		5	9
			8		3			1	
6				7		9		8	5
	2				6	5	7		
14	21	17	34	17	24	32	28	17	21

Kropki

Place each number from 1 to 8 once each into every row and column. Squares separated by a black dot must contain numbers where one is equal to twice the value of the other. Squares separated by a white dot must contain consecutive numbers – i.e. where the difference in value between them is 1. All possible dots are given. If a 1 and 2 are in touching squares, they may be separated by *either* a black or a white dot.

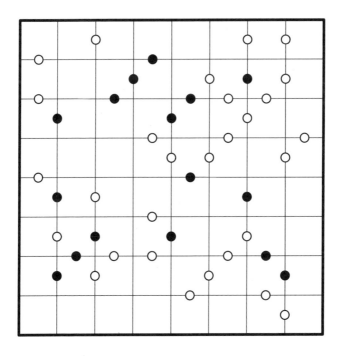

Hints and Tips

Guessing and Experimentation

» Have you ever thought to yourself, "I can't do that", when faced with an unfamiliar task? As we age, our childhood fearlessness begins to be replaced by a fear of failure. This fear then often inhibits us from trying new things. Luckily, it's possible to help overcome these fears by using some simple techniques, such as deliberately guessing when you don't know what to do next. This process is similar to how you first learned to walk: by taking experimental steps and then building on top of what you learned from them.

» Using experimentation or guesswork in an attempt to solve a puzzle or learn a task may seem incredibly daunting, since it is natural to be afraid of "failure". But, instead of worrying about the opinions of yourself or others, try to see experimentation as a valuable technique to help you learn about something much more quickly than you could via any other method. Of course, that said, it's best to use the experimental method in a situation where failure has no damaging consequences.

» When guessing, use your common sense to find a sensible place to start, and then explore that guess to see what the result is. If you're lucky, you'll make a guess which will quickly lead to a contradiction or problem, should it have been incorrect or a poor guess. And then, even though the guess was wrong, the knowledge gained from the initial guess will help you improve your next guess. Every step – even missteps – can help you figure out how to do things better next time.

» A system of trial and error, by which you are willing to fail through a process of experimentation, is useful in many aspects of life. It is usually better to do something, even if you get it wrong, than simply not to do anything at all. For example, next time you're stuck on a puzzle, just try guessing to help you get going. You never know what you might learn from the result of that guess.

Tren

Draw 1×2 and 1×3 rectangular blocks along the grid lines so that each number is contained in exactly one block. The number in each block reveals the total count of all of the white spaces that the block can slide into. Shapes that are wider than they are tall slide only horizontally left and right, and shapes that are taller than they are wide slide only vertically up and down.

See the example solution above to understand how this works. For example, consider the 2 in the top row – it can move into 2 spaces. Meanwhile, the 0 at the bottom right cannot move into any spaces; the spaces above it do not count because it does not slide this way.

		4			1		1
1				2			
	3		5				
4							2
							3
						1	
		2		3			0
		2		0			

King's Journey

Write a number in each empty square so that every number from 1 to 64 appears once each in the grid. The numbers must form a continuous path, so you can move from square to touching square to journey from 1 all the way up to 64. Squares count as touching if they are immediately to the left, right, top or bottom of a square, or if they touch diagonally.

	16	18	19		22		
							29
	10		5		25		31
9	7			1		34	
	8		3		38		36
		60				41	
		52					
	57		64		48	44	

Easy as A, B, C

Place the letters A, B and C once each into every row and column of the grid. This means that two squares in each row and column will remain empty.

Letters given outside the grid reveal the letter that is encountered first when reading along that row or column from the given letter.

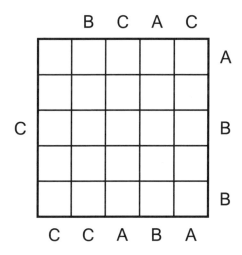

Masyu

Draw a single loop that travels through the middle of some squares, using only horizontal and vertical lines. The loop must visit all of the circles.

The loop must make a 90-degree turn in all squares with a shaded circle, and then pass straight through the next square on both sides of the turn (i.e. may not turn in the immediately following or preceding square). Conversely, the loop must pass straight through a white circle without turning, but it must turn in at least one of the preceding or following squares.

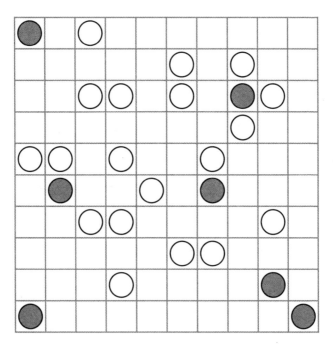

No Four in a Row

Can you complete this grid by placing either an O or an ✕ into each empty square? You must place the symbols so that *no* lines of four or more of the same symbol are made in any direction, including diagonally.

O	O			✕	O	✕		O
O			✕	✕	O	✕		
			✕	O		O	✕	O
O	O	O		O		O		O
✕								✕
			✕	O		✕		O
✕	O	✕					✕	✕
✕			✕	O		O	✕	
O	✕		O	O	✕		✕	✕

Quad Fit

Place a digit from 1 to 7 into every square so that each digit appears once in every row and column.

Groups of four digits are placed on the intersection of some sets of four squares. These four digits must be placed, once each, into the four squares that surround the group. They are sorted into numerical order, so it is up to you to work out which square each one must go in.

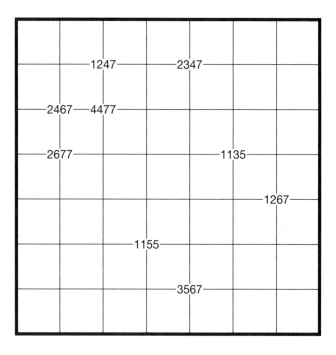

Creative Pixels

The empty boxes below are just waiting to be filled in – but what should go in them? Well, that's up to you. You could shade them to make some "pixel art". You could create perhaps an arcade ghost, or a smiley face, or maybe a flower. Or perhaps you should write letters in some of the boxes. You could even shade them at random, or in a pattern, and see what results. It's entirely up to you. There is no "right" or "wrong" answer to this puzzle.

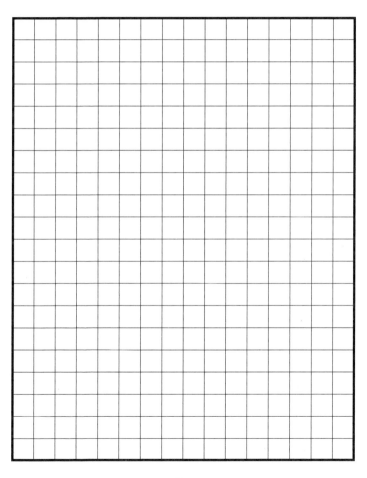

Touchy

Place the letters from A to H into the empty squares, so that each letter appears once in every row and column. Identical letters cannot touch – not even diagonally.

	H	F			A	G	
E							D
D							F
		G	D				
		A	F				
F							H
B							C
	D	H			E	B	

Jigsaw

Place a letter from A to G into the empty squares, so that each letter appears once in every row, column and bold-lined jigsaw shape.

	D			E		
					G	
	B					
			G			
					F	
	E					
		F			C	

Frame Sudoku

Place 1 to 9 once each into every row, column and bold-lined 3×3 box. Numbers outside the grid give the sum of the three nearest numbers in the same row or column.

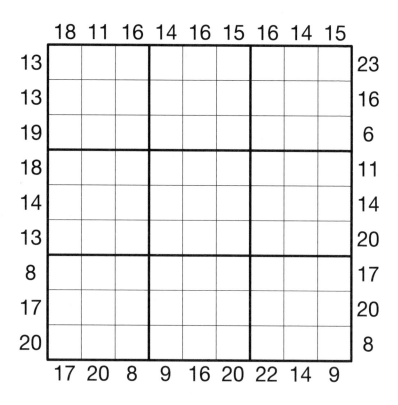

Rectangles

Draw along some of the dashed lines to divide the grid up into a set of squares and rectangles, so that every shape contains exactly one number. The printed number contained within each shape must be exactly equal to the number of grid squares within that shape.

All grid squares must belong to exactly one square or one rectangle.

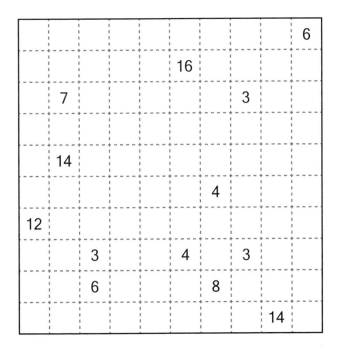

Hints and Tips

Innate Responses

» Your brain is an incredible computing powerhouse. There are constantly a huge number of mental processes going on that your conscious mind is not even aware of – but which are fundamental to your very being. For example, when you speak, how do you decide what to say? Much of your spoken language is produced by a team effort between the conscious and unconscious parts of your brain. This is why you may sometimes find yourself blurting out something that may not have been your first choice of words. The unconscious part of your brain supplied the words, and only as you spoke them did you stop to consciously think about their exact implications. While you could stop and rehearse everything you wanted to say before uttering it, this would make for very stilted conversation, so the brain's actions are a sensible compromise.

» Despite their phenomenal prowess, our brains do have some unhelpful and evolutionarily primitive responses that are not always relevant in modern life. One in particular is that it is instinctive to go along with the rest of a group, even if they aren't acting sensibly – and in psychological tests, most people will give an answer they know is wrong if other people have first given a false answer. This type of response is especially prevalent in stressful situations, so when people aren't sure what to do they look around to see what other people are doing. This isn't always helpful.

» Our innate responses can also create a false sense of urgency, based on our primitive need to secure food sources, which leads to a fear of losing out that can often outweigh a more considered and rational approach. A good example of this is being swayed by Black Friday sales. Research has shown that it is, in fact, generally cheaper to purchase products at other times of the year, yet their sense of false urgency leads people to make irrational choices and buy things they would otherwise not have done. If a sign claims to offer a "70% reduction", our brain thinks that it is an opportunity that simply cannot be missed. And yet if you take a moment to think about whether you really need the item, or whether you are certain that it really is a good deal, you may well come to a conclusion different from your initial, innate response.

Wordoku

Place a letter in each square so that there are nine different letters in the grid, and no letter repeats in any row, column or bold-lined 3×3 box.

When you are finished, a word will be spelled along the shaded diagonal.

		C			I	T		
I					O	N		
N			T		D			
T		D						
C		I				U		D
						C		E
		D		A				T
		N	E					U
		E	I			A		

Circular Pairs

Draw straight horizontal or vertical lines to join each white circle to exactly one shaded circle.

Lines cannot cross over either another line or over a circle.

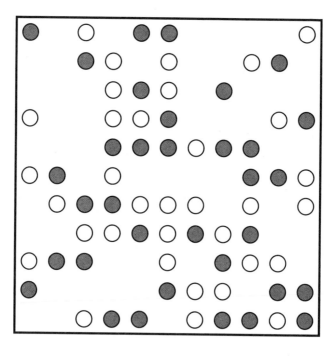

LITS

Shade some squares to create one tetromino within each bold-lined area. A tetromino is a shape made up of four adjacently touching squares. Tetrominoes must be L, I, T or S shapes, but not a solid 2×2 box, so these are the four options:

All shaded squares in the puzzle must form a single connected area, as in the example solution to the right. Conversely, there must not be any shaded areas of 2×2 squares (or larger).

No two of the same type of tetromino (L, I, T or S) may touch, except diagonally. Reflections and rotations of the same type of tetromino still count as the same tetromino, and therefore may not touch one another.

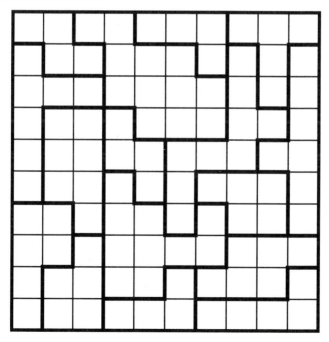

Sudoku

Place a digit from 1 to 9 into every empty square so that each digit appears once in every row, column and bold-lined 3×3 box.

2								6
		1	2	4	7	5		
	4						1	
	1		5		8		3	
	3			2			8	
	5		1		4		7	
	9						5	
		7	6	5	1	3		
3								1

Loop Finder

Draw a single loop that visits every white square. The loop can travel only horizontally or vertically between touching white squares, and cannot cross over itself or enter any square more than once.

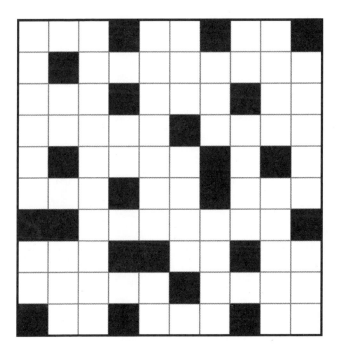

Killer Sudoku

Place a digit from 1 to 9 into every square so that each digit appears once in every row, column and bold-lined 3×3 box.

Digits in each dashed-line cage must add together to give the total printed at the top-left of that dashed-line cage. Digits cannot be repeated within any individual dashed-line cage.

Number Link

Draw ten paths in the grid, each joining a pair of identical numbers. The lines must pass horizontally or vertically between the middles of touching squares, and cannot cross or touch at any point.

1	2		3					
4						5		
	6			5	7			
					3			
	6						8	
		4		2	7	9		
10	1				10	8		
				9				

Fences

Can you complete this fence, by connecting exactly two fence panels to each fence post? Fences are represented by either horizontal or vertical lines, and some are drawn in already.

The finished fence must form a single loop that visits every post once.

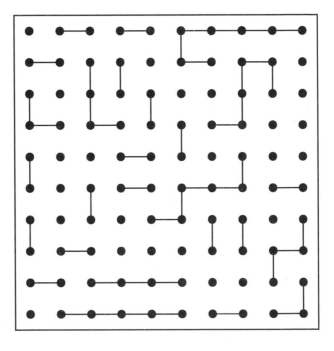

Binary Numbers

Write either a 0 or a 1 into each empty square, so that each row and each column contains five 0s and five 1s.

The numbers must be written so that no more than two of any number occur immediately next to one another within any row or column. For example, "01001101" would be fine, but "01000110" would not, due to the three 0s in immediate succession.

			0					0	1
		0							1
				0	1		1		
	0		0						
			0					0	
1				0	1				
1		0							0
		1			1		1		
1					0	0		0	0
1	1						0		

Nurikabe

Shade some of the empty squares so that each number remains in an unshaded region of the given number of squares. There must be exactly one number in each unshaded region in the completed puzzle.

Shaded squares cannot form any 2×2 (or larger) areas, and all shaded squares must also form a single continuous region.

Regions count as continuous if squares touch to the left, right, above or below – but not diagonally.

	2		1			2		1	
									2
		5							
				4					
			1						
					2				
	2								5
			4			2			

Jigsaw

Place a letter from A to G into the empty squares, so that each letter appears once in every row, column and bold-lined jigsaw shape.

				C		
		A			F	
E					G	
		A				
	E					B
	D			A		
		D				

Hints and Tips

Fresh Perspectives

»   Sometimes it's helpful to try and get a fresh perspective on a problem. We've already looked at how some puzzles can be tackled by making a guess to get you started, but this isn't always appropriate.

»   When you start on a problem, it is easy to make some initial assumptions which then go unchallenged. If those initial assumptions were not helpful, you might then be unable to make any progress, no matter how creatively you think about a solution. This is because it is difficult to escape your own preconceptions, and see things from a different angle.

»   One way to help gain a fresh perspective on a problem is to talk to other people who may have a different view. Often the more people the better, so long as everyone is given a chance to speak. And sometimes, simply explaining what the problem actually *is* to someone can help you make progress – what is "obvious" to you may not be obvious to them, and perhaps it is actually not quite so obvious as you first thought.

»   Different people think in different ways, and it is only natural to be tempted to stick to your own ideas – even when they are no longer serving you well. Hearing someone else's outlook, even if their ideas seem ridiculous, can often lead to a fresh way of thinking – even if that breakthrough doesn't happen immediately. Use other people to bounce ideas off, and see what they say. They may not have the solution, but they might help you make progress in the process.

Walls

Draw either a horizontal or a vertical line in each empty square, so that each line passes through the middle of the square and runs the full width or height of the square. In this way, runs of horizontal lines in horizontally adjacent squares form a single longer line that passes through multiple squares, and similarly for vertical lines in vertically adjacent squares.

Numbered squares in the grid reveal the total length of all the lines that touch those squares, measured in terms of the number of grid squares the line passes through.

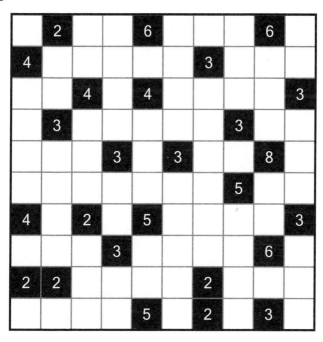

Spiral Galaxies

In this unusual puzzle, the aim is to draw along the grid lines to form a rotationally symmetrical shape around each of the circular "pivots" marked in the puzzle. All of the shapes must be drawn so that they could be rotated 180 degrees around their pivots and yet still look identical.

The shapes must be placed so that every square in the grid is part of exactly one shape. This means that shapes cannot overlap.

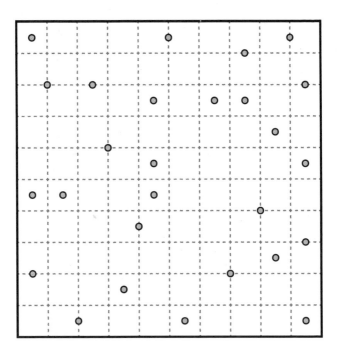

Meadows

Draw along the dashed grid lines to divide this "meadow" up into a number of squares, of size 1x1 or larger, so that every region formed in the grid is a perfect square – and there are no grid squares left over that are not part of any shape.

Each region must contain exactly one "cow". The cows are represented by circles.

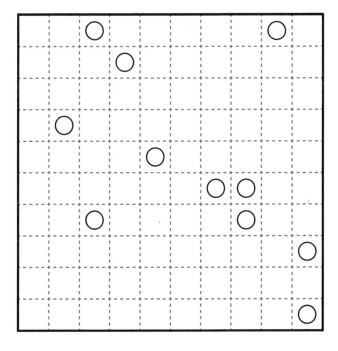

Lighthouses

Place ships in some of the grid squares, so that every ship is lit by at least one lighthouse. Lighthouses are the numbered, black squares. Lighthouses illuminate all squares in the same row or column, irrespective of whether another ship or lighthouse is in the way.

Each lighthouse must light up the given number of ships. Also, ships cannot touch either each other or a lighthouse – not even diagonally.

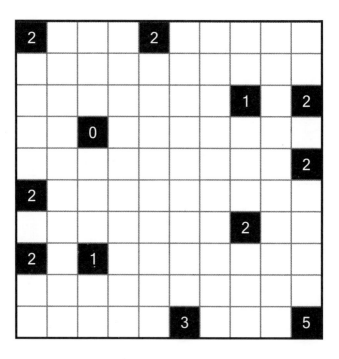

Clouds

Shade grid squares to form rectangular "clouds" of 2×2 squares or larger. Clouds cannot touch – not even diagonally.

Numbers outside the grid give the total number of shaded grid squares in their corresponding row or column.

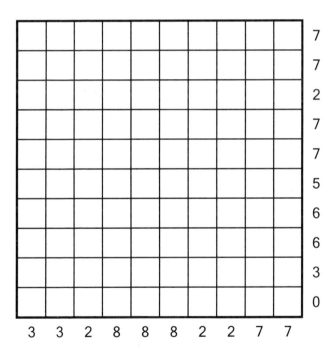

Samurai Sudoku

Place a digit from 1 to 6 into every empty square so that each digit appears once in every row, column and bold-lined 2×3 box of the three overlapping 6×6 sudoku grids. The grids must be solved together in order to reach a unique solution.

Zigzag

Test your vocabulary by completing this zigzag puzzle. The aim is to write a letter in each shaded box in order to form a complete eight-letter word on each row.

The last two letters of each row also form the first two letters of the following row, in the same order. These connections are indicated visually by the diagonal lines.

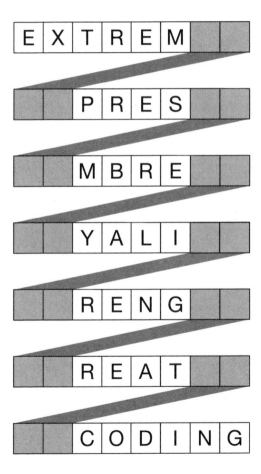

Word Pyramid

Can you complete this word pyramid by solving the clues, placing one letter per square? Each row will contain the exact same letters as the previous row, plus the addition of one extra letter – although the order of the letters may be rearranged.

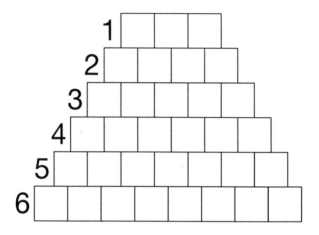

1. Large

2. Insult; mocking remark

3. Start

4. Gentle and kind

5. Shaping into a curve

6. Mixing together

Link Words

Each of the following pairs of words secretly conceals a third word. This third word can be added to the end of the first word, and the start of the second word, to form two new words.

Can you reveal all six hidden words? For example, GRID _____ SMITH would be hiding the word LOCK, to make GRIDLOCK and LOCKSMITH.

OUT   _ _ _   SACK

PUT   _ _ _   DANCE

SWORD   _ _ _ _   TAIL

CLOCK   _ _ _ _   CRACK

COUNTER   _ _ _ _   RIDGE

Bridges

Draw horizontal and vertical lines to join pairs of numbers, so that all the numbers connect together to form one large connected set. This means that you can start on any number and follow lines to reach any other number.

Lines cannot cross over either another line or over a number, and each number must have the exact number of connecting lines given.

There can be no more than two lines joining any given pair of numbers.

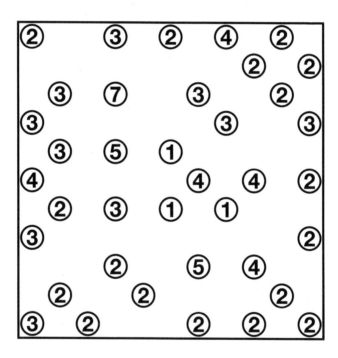

Kropki

Place each number from 1 to 8 once each into every row and column. Squares separated by a black dot must contain numbers where one is equal to twice the value of the other. Squares separated by a white dot must contain consecutive numbers – i.e. where the difference in value between them is 1. All possible dots are given. If a 1 and 2 are in touching squares, they may be separated by *either* a black or a white dot.

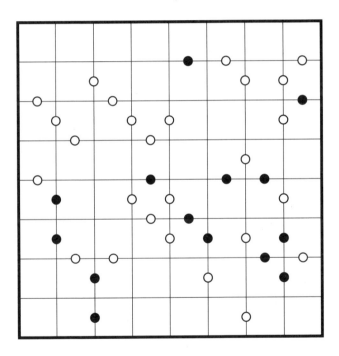

Hints and Tips

Getting Comfortable with Numbers

» Try as we might, we cannot escape numbers. They are everywhere in our daily lives, from grocery shopping receipts to the number of days left to a deadline – or holiday. Despite this, many people claim an aversion to numbers, claiming they "can't do numbers". The truth is, of course, that *everyone* can understand numbers to a certain extent, and real-life mathematics is often far away from images of high-school algebra.

» The type of number calculations we need in our day-to-day lives, such as checking a restaurant total or a checkout receipt value, can often be done with the basic estimation skills we all possess. Make an effort to try and work out rough predictions of how much you are about to spend, so you can start using your innate mathematical abilities. Forget about the decimal components, and simply round numbers to get to a quick total.

» Doing mathematics in your head might feel stressful, or even like an impossible task. However, like all skills it does become easier with practice, as you start to learn to hold numbers in your head and manipulate them – without forgetting where you are in your calculation. What's more, this is not only excellent brain training but can help improve your quality of life too. Try doing numbers in your head by adding up your shopping cart as you go.

» It is worthwhile to take some time to refresh your memory by relearning your times tables – or rehearsing the parts you were always fuzzy on. Multiplications are involved in all aspects of life, such as when calculating if a multi-buy discount really is good value or not. Having a ready familiarity with multiples up to 10× is all you really need – most calculations don't require you to know higher tables.

Bricks

Try these gentle number-based puzzles, where the aim is to write a number from 1 to 6 into each empty square so that each bold-lined area of two squares contains one even and one odd number. Additionally, no number can appear more than once in any row or column.

1		4			
	1	2		6	
	3		4		
				2	4
			6	4	
6					1

5					
	4	3		5	
	5				
	3	6		4	
		4	3	6	
3					6

Number Wall

Test your number skills by writing a number from 0 to 9 into every empty square of this numerical wall.

Numbers must be placed so that each column of white squares adds up to the value given in the bottom, shaded square of that column. For example, the five white squares in the first column must sum to a total of 22.

Identical numbers cannot touch – not even diagonally.

Finally, a number cannot repeat within a single row. This means that every row must contain each number from 0 to 9 exactly once each. Note that numbers *can* repeat within a column, subject to the no-touching rule.

4				3	5				7
	2			6		9			8
		7		4			8		9
0	4		8						7
				2		4	5		
22	17	25	31	21	19	20	19	20	31

Brain Chains

Mental arithmetic skills are incredibly important in everyday life, whether you're making sure you aren't being overcharged when shopping, or working out what to pay when you have to split a restaurant bill. For practice, try solving all of these brain chain puzzles without making any written notes – that is, just in your head. For each chain, follow every step in turn from the given number until you reach the final result. Write this number in the box at the end of the chain.

| 8 | +1 | ×1/3 | ×6 | +40 | -19 | RESULT |

| 37 | ×2 | -11 | ÷3 | ×1/3 | ×4 | RESULT |

| 41 | -17 | +53 | -27 | ÷5 | +50% | RESULT |

| 33 | +34 | -21 | ÷2 | -8 | +40% | RESULT |

| 48 | +59 | -76 | ×3 | +87 | ÷5 | RESULT |

Number Pyramid

Write a number in each empty block in this pyramid. The numbers must be chosen so that every block contains a value equal to the sum of the two blocks immediately beneath it.

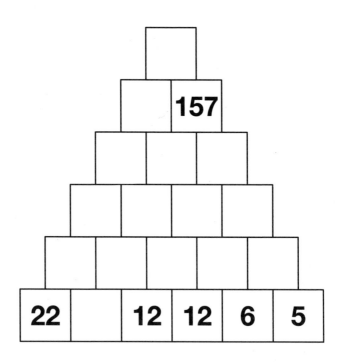

Jigsaw

Place a letter from A to G into the empty squares, so that each letter appears once in every row, column and bold-lined jigsaw shape.

C					D	
	A	G				
					F	
	D					
				C	B	
	F					D

Quad Fit

Place a digit from 1 to 7 into every square so that each digit appears once in every row and column.

Groups of four digits are placed on the intersection of some sets of four squares. These four digits must be placed, once each, into the four squares that surround the group. They are sorted into numerical order, so it is up to you to work out which square each one must go in.

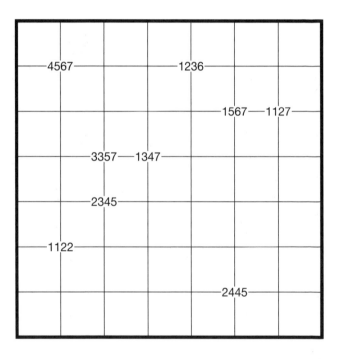

★★

Cube Folding

Imagine cutting out each of these shapes below, and then folding inward along the black lines. Some of them could be folded into six-sided cubes, but some could not. Circle the one, or ones, that would not form complete cubes.

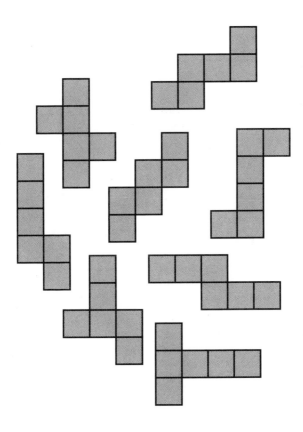

Touchy

Place the letters from A to H into the empty squares, so that each letter appears once in every row and column. Identical letters cannot touch – not even diagonally.

D							G
			C	A			
		B			F		
	H		G	B		D	
	D		H	C		A	
		C			B		
			F	G			
E							B

Calcudoku

Place a number from 1 to 7 in each square so that each number appears once in every row and column. Also, the numbers in each bold-lined region must result in the number given at the top left when the given operation is applied between all the numbers in that region. For subtraction and division, start with the highest number in the region and then subtract or divide by the remaining numbers.

2÷		6÷	28×		21+	
4+			126×		336×	
8×	16+					
		90×				8+
1470×		1−				
		1−		6+	3+	
					2÷	

Frame Sudoku

Place 1 to 9 once each into every row, column and bold-lined 3×3 box. Numbers outside the grid give the sum of the three nearest numbers in the same row or column.

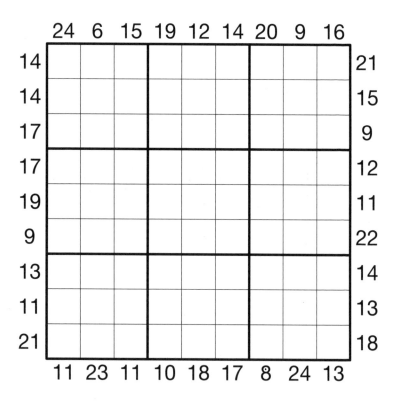

★★

Futoshiki

Place a digit from 1 to 7 into each empty square, so that each digit appears once in every row and column. You must place the numbers so they obey the inequality signs between some squares. The arrow always points to the smaller of the two numbers.

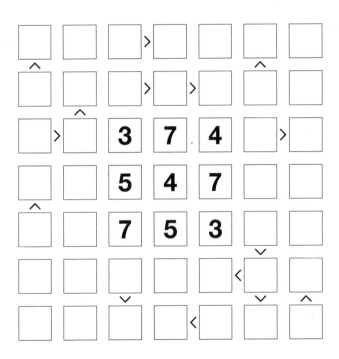

Hints and Tips

Memory

» Your brain is constantly processing a phenomenal amount of information from all of your senses throughout the day. It makes sense that you will never remember most of this vast stream of information, and even things you *want* to recall can be difficult to remember. Luckily, there are certain tips and techniques that you can use when you want to increase your chance of remembering something.

» Paying attention and focusing on what you want to remember is the first and most important key element of memory. If you haven't noticed something, you can't remember it; and if it didn't seem important to you, why should your brain bother to remember it?

» Learning a list of facts can be tough, but your brain is better at it than you realize – sometimes it just needs some help! For example, when you're trying to learn facts, group them together into interrelated elements. It is much easier to learn information in connected groups than as individual facts.

» Using association is a helpful tool when trying to memorize something. Connecting information with strong emotions, other memories or vibrant images can make it easier to recall them at a later stage. Forming these connections helps create alternative recall routes that make your memories more accessible, and therefore easier to "find" when you need to retrieve them.

» For short lists or sets of items, you can help yourself memorize them by using a mnemonic technique. You take the initials of each word of a set of items and then use those initials to form a quirky expression. For example, the order of the rainbow can be remembered through the sentence "Richard Of York Gave Battle In Vain." It's up to you to convert the initial letters, "R O Y G B I V", back into "red, orange, yellow...", but if it's just the order you need to remember, this simple phrase can be a useful aide-memoire. Try creating new mnemonics for information you don't want to forget.

Memory Test

Take a look at the following list of vegetables for up to 30 seconds, then cover it over and write as many of them as possible on the empty list at the bottom of the page. The first letter of each vegetable will, however, be given as a memory aid.

Cabbage	Carrot	Mushroom
Artichoke	Potato	Squash
Cucumber	Lettuce	Kale
Leek	Broccoli	Onion

Now cover over the top half of the page and write down as many of the vegetables as possible:

C_____	C_____	M_____
A_____	P_____	S_____
C_____	L_____	K_____
L_____	B_____	O_____

How did you do? If you didn't remember them all, go back and repeat the exercise and see if it helps you remember the remaining words.

Bridges

Draw horizontal and vertical lines to join pairs of numbers, so that all the numbers connect together to form one large connected set. This means that you can start on any number and follow lines to reach any other number.

Lines cannot cross over either another line or over a number, and each number must have the exact number of connecting lines given.

There can be no more than two lines joining any given pair of numbers.

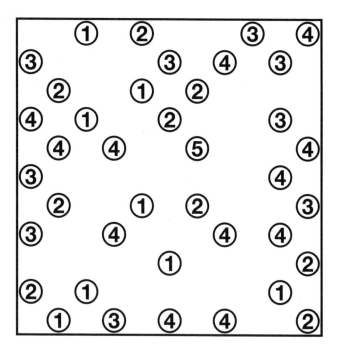

Kropki

Place each number from 1 to 8 once each into every row and column. Squares separated by a black dot must contain numbers where one is equal to twice the value of the other. Squares separated by a white dot must contain consecutive numbers – i.e. where the difference in value between them is 1. All possible dots are given. If a 1 and 2 are in touching squares, they may be separated by *either* a black or a white dot.

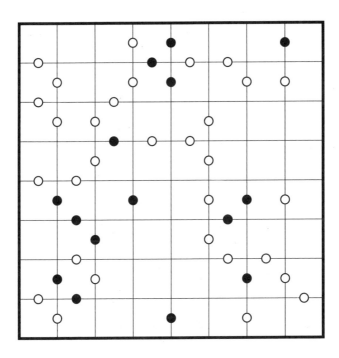

Sudoku

Place a digit from 1 to 9 into every empty square so that each digit appears once in every row, column and bold-lined 3×3 box.

6			7		9			3
			8		2			
		4		5		6		
4	6						1	8
		7		2		3		
9	5						6	7
		5		3		9		
			4		8			
2			6		5			1

Number Link

Draw ten paths in the grid, each joining a pair of identical numbers. The lines must pass horizontally or vertically between the middles of touching squares, and cannot cross or touch at any point.

	1		2	3	4			
	5		6				7	
			8					
								4
						3		
1		7						
5			2					
		9				6		
	10			10			8	
					9			

Killer Sudoku

Place a digit from 1 to 9 into every square so that each digit appears once in every row, column and bold-lined 3×3 box.

Digits in each dashed-line cage must add together to give the total printed at the top-left of that dashed-line cage. Digits cannot be repeated within any individual dashed-line cage.

Fences

Can you complete this fence, by connecting exactly two fence panels to each fence post? Fences are represented by either horizontal or vertical lines, and some are drawn in already.

The finished fence must form a single loop that visits every post once.

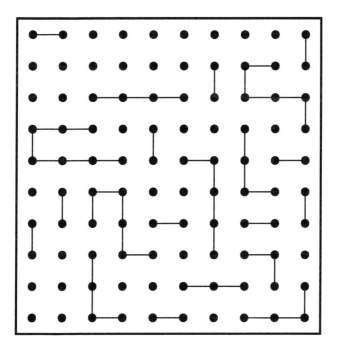

King's Journey

Write a number in each empty square so that every number from 1 to 64 appears once each in the grid. The numbers must form a continuous path, so you can move from square to touching square to journey from 1 all the way up to 64. Squares count as touching if they are immediately to the left, right, top or bottom of a square, or if they touch diagonally.

10		8	57		54	50	51
		7		58			
12		46	44			63	
	4				64		62
3					42		24
2		36	38	39			
1			20	33			
	18				32		29

Easy as A, B, C

Place the letters A, B and C once each into every row and column of the grid. This means that two squares in each row and column will remain empty.

Letters given outside the grid reveal the letter that is encountered first when reading along that row or column from the given letter.

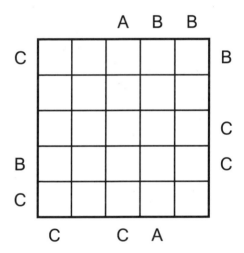

Light Up

Draw light bulbs in some of the squares so that every white square is lit. Light bulbs illuminate all squares in the same row or column until the first black square they encounter – i.e. light does not pass through the black squares. Light bulbs cannot illuminate one another, although more than one light bulb may illuminate an empty square.

Squares with numbers must contain that many light bulbs in the adjacent squares (i.e. squares touching to the left, right, above or below). Not all light bulbs are necessarily indicated by number clues, however.

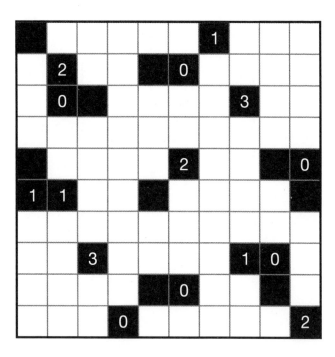

Shaded Rooms

Shade some of the grid squares in such a way that no two shaded squares touch one another – except diagonally – and so that all unshaded squares form a single continuous area.

Numbered squares may or may not be shaded, but always give the exact amount of shaded squares in a bold-lined room.

Any continuous horizontal or vertical run of unshaded squares cannot cross more than one bold line.

0	4						0		
				0					
0					3				1
	1								
2									
		1							
0	2			3		1	0		
							2		

Hints and Tips

Improving Communication

» Knowing how to communicate clearly has obvious benefits, such as being able to adequately express your ideas – or even to form meaningful relationships. However, having good communication skills has an additional benefit that may not be obvious, since it will also help you think with improved clarity. The more you can express concepts in a compact and meaningful way, the better you will be able to manage thoughts that revolve around those concepts.

» It's always worth trying to improve your communication skills. They shouldn't be something you learned once, a long time ago, but are instead a lifelong task that is constantly evolving. Aim to expand your vocabulary wherever possible, and read as widely as you can.

» Reading can be either of fact or fiction, and in both cases aim to expose yourself to a wide range of views. With fiction, try reading a broad range of genres, or read factual reports from opposing sources and viewpoints. What's more, reading is an easy thing to do, and which you can spend as long – or as little – a time on as you like.

» Another route to improve your word skills is to challenge yourself with crosswords or other word-based puzzles. Crosswords are largely vocabulary-based, and regularly tackling these puzzles can be a fun and interesting way to improve your vocabulary. They might seem tough when first tackled, but if you aren't a big word-puzzle fan, it's worth persevering – they get easier with practice!

Line Sweeper

Draw a loop that passes through the middle of some squares, using only horizontal and vertical lines. The loop can enter each square only once, and so cannot touch or cross over itself at any point.

Numbers in the grid reveal the number of touching squares that the loop enters, including diagonally touching squares.

3				3			
				5			
		7					3
		6					
					6		
5		5			5		
						7	

Masyu

Draw a single loop that travels through the middle of some squares, using only horizontal and vertical lines. The loop must visit all of the circles.

The loop must make a 90-degree turn in all squares with a shaded circle, and then pass straight through the next square on both sides of the turn (i.e. may not turn in the immediately following or preceding square). Conversely, the loop must pass straight through a white circle without turning, but it must turn in at least one of the preceding or following squares.

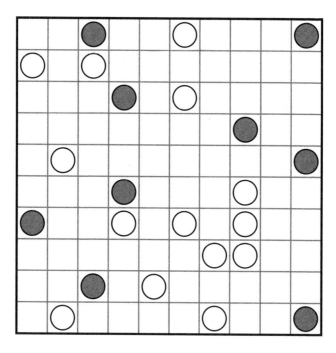

Tren

Draw 1×2 and 1×3 rectangular blocks along the grid lines so that each number is contained in exactly one block. The number in each block reveals the total count of all of the white spaces that the block can slide into. Shapes that are wider than they are tall slide only horizontally left and right, and shapes that are taller than they are wide slide only vertically up and down.

See the example solution above to understand how this works. For example consider the 2 in the top row – it can move into 2 spaces. Meanwhile, the 0 at the bottom right cannot move into any spaces; the spaces above it do not count because it does not slide this way.

			4			1	
	1						2
		5		0		0	
	4				2		2
1				2			
			4				
0			1			0	

Ripple Effect

Place a digit into each empty square so that every bold-lined region contains each digit from 1 up to and including the number of squares in that region. For example, a 4-square region must contain the digits 1, 2, 3 and 4.

Also, no digit can be placed so that it is within that many squares of an identical digit in either a horizontal or vertical direction. This means, for a digit x, that there must be at least x squares (which do not contain the digit x) between that digit and any other occurrence of that digit in the same row or column.

2		3		2	1		1
	1		5				2
1					2		1
	3		1	2		5	3
	1	5		3	4		
1			4	5		1	
3		2			2	3	1
		1		1			3

LITS

Shade some squares to create one tetromino within each bold-lined area. A tetromino is a shape made up of four adjacently touching squares. Tetrominoes must be L, I, T or S shapes, but not a solid 2×2 box, so these are the four options:

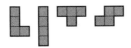

All shaded squares in the puzzle must form a single connected area, as in the example solution to the right. Conversely, there must not be any shaded areas of 2×2 squares (or larger).

No two of the same type of tetromino (L, I, T or S) may touch, except diagonally. Reflections and rotations of the same type of tetromino still count as the same tetromino, and therefore may not touch one another.

Samurai Sudoku

Place a digit from 1 to 6 into every empty square so that each digit appears once in every row, column and bold-lined 2×3 box of the three overlapping 6×6 sudoku grids. The grids must be solved together in order to reach a unique solution.

Walls

Draw either a horizontal or a vertical line in each empty square, so that each line passes through the middle of the square and runs the full width or height of the square. In this way, runs of horizontal lines in horizontally adjacent squares form a single longer line that passes through multiple squares, and similarly for vertical lines in vertically adjacent squares.

Numbered squares in the grid reveal the total length of all the lines that touch those squares, measured in terms of the number of grid squares the line passes through.

		8		4				6	
1						5			
5			5						3
					5				
			2			5			
	7								1
		6		6		4			
	7					4		2	
5					1				
	6		4				2		

Spiral Galaxies

In this unusual puzzle, the aim is to draw along the grid lines to form a rotationally symmetrical shape around each of the circular "pivots" marked in the puzzle. All of the shapes must be drawn so that they could be rotated 180 degrees around their pivots and yet still look identical.

The shapes must be placed so that every square in the grid is part of exactly one shape. This means that shapes cannot overlap.

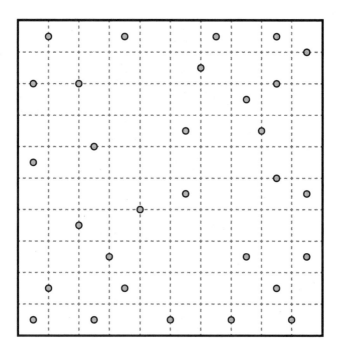

Touchy

Place the letters from A to H into the empty squares, so that each letter appears once in every row and column. Identical letters cannot touch – not even diagonally.

		H			C		
			A	D			
B							D
	H		E	G		B	
	D		C	A		H	
E							G
			F	E			
		D			A		

Circular Pairs

Draw straight horizontal or vertical lines to join each white circle to exactly one shaded circle.

Lines cannot cross over either another line or over a circle.

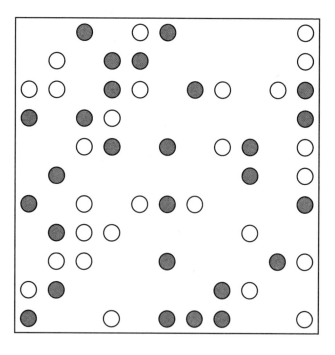

Clouds

Shade grid squares to form rectangular "clouds" of 2×2 squares or larger. Clouds cannot touch – not even diagonally.

Numbers outside the grid give the total number of shaded grid squares in their corresponding row or column.

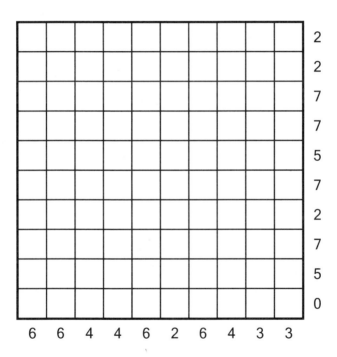

Hints and Tips

The Genius Question

» What is a "genius"? It is someone with an outstanding ability at something, which appears to everyone else as an incredible natural talent. But, while someone with extraordinary abilities may have a particular aptitude, in reality what distinguishes them most of all is that they have gone above and beyond their peers by putting in the time and effort to reach their special level. So, no matter what your particular talents, the chances are that you have the germ of a genius inside you – at whatever activities you are particularly skilled at.

» It is easier to become an expert at something when you start at a young age, but this shouldn't discourage you as an adult. It is sometimes claimed that it takes 10,000 hours of practice to become expert at something, but this is clearly a huge approximation since it depends on both the activity and the person. But the key point is that it takes a *lot* of time and practice – it won't happen overnight.

» Try thinking about something you have always wanted to learn, or something you know about but have always wanted to take to the next step. Consider making a concerted effort to learn or develop that activity, and don't give up. To help motivate you, try recording your progression as you go. You might be pleasantly surprised at how much you progress, since often we don't recognize the progress we make because it happens over time and we forget where we once were – whereas a friend who hasn't seen us in a year would see it immediately. Tracking your progress will give you an objective assessment of your own improvement.

Sets

Draw along some of the dashed lines to divide the grid up into 12 separate regions, each containing the letters A to F exactly once.

B	B	D	E	C	E	A	F
D	A	E	F	D	F	B	C
E	E	C	C	A	D	A	D
F	A	F	C	F	A	C	B
B	D	B	B	A	C	F	A
A	D	C	D	E	F	E	B
F	C	B	A	D	E	B	D
E	B	F	C	D	D	E	C
A	E	F	C	A	B	F	E

Binary Numbers

Write either a 0 or a 1 into each empty square, so that each row and each column contains five 0s and five 1s.

The numbers must be written so that no more than two of any number occur immediately next to one another within any row or column. For example, "01001101" would be fine, but "01000110" would not, due to the three 0s in immediate succession.

0	0		0			1			
	0	0		0					1
			1	1				0	0
		0					0		
			1			1			0
			0	1		1		1	1
		0							
						1		1	
1					0				0
1		0	1		0				

Loop Finder

Draw a single loop that visits every white square. The loop can travel only horizontally or vertically between touching white squares, and cannot cross over itself or enter any square more than once.

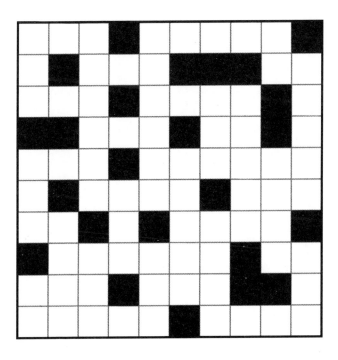

No Four in a Row

Can you complete this grid by placing either an O or an × into each empty square? You must place the symbols so that *no* lines of four or more of the same symbol are made in any direction, including diagonally.

×		×		×		O		×
O	×			×				×
	O		O	×		×		×
O	O		O			×		O
	O			×			×	
O			O		×	O		O
O	O		O			O	O	O
O	O		O	O			O	O
	×			×		×	O	

Zigzag

Test your vocabulary by completing this zigzag puzzle. The aim is to write a letter in each shaded box in order to form a complete eight-letter word on each row.

The last two letters of each row also form the first two letters of the following row, in the same order. These connections are indicated visually by the diagonal lines.

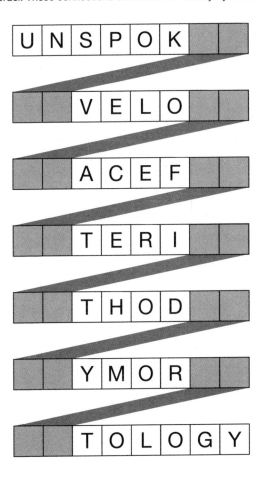

Quad Fit

Place a digit from 1 to 7 into every square so that each digit appears once in every row and column.

Groups of four digits are placed on the intersection of some sets of four squares. These four digits must be placed, once each, into the four squares that surround the group. They are sorted into numerical order, so it is up to you to work out which square each one must go in.

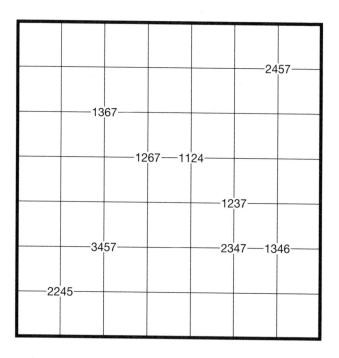

★

Rectangles

Draw along some of the dashed lines to divide the grid up into a set of squares and rectangles, so that every shape contains exactly one number. The printed number contained within each shape must be exactly equal to the number of grid squares within that shape.

All grid squares must belong to exactly one square or one rectangle.

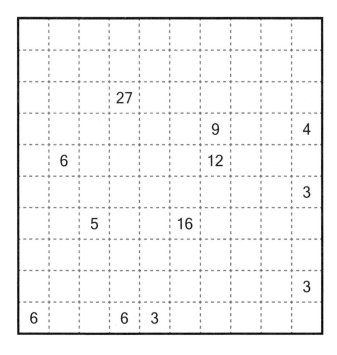

Fences

Can you complete this fence, by connecting exactly two fence panels to each fence post? Fences are represented by either horizontal or vertical lines, and some are drawn in already.

The finished fence must form a single loop that visits every post once.

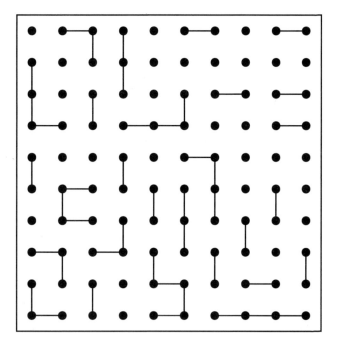

Shaded Rooms

Shade some of the grid squares in such a way that no two shaded squares touch one another – except diagonally – and so that all unshaded squares form a single continuous area.

Numbered squares may or may not be shaded, but always give the exact amount of shaded squares in a bold-lined room.

Any continuous horizontal or vertical run of unshaded squares cannot cross more than one bold line.

1		3		1			2		
2	0						1		
	2			2			1	3	
					1				
					2				
	4		2						
					1	0			

King's Journey

Write a number in each empty square so that every number from 1 to 64 appears once each in the grid. The numbers must form a continuous path, so you can move from square to touching square to journey from 1 all the way up to 64. Squares count as touching if they are immediately to the left, right, top or bottom of a square, or if they touch diagonally.

7	8	9		11	1	15	
		10				13	
		35	32				18
40	38						
45						26	
				29			21
63	64		56	49			22
				52			

Line Sweeper

Draw a loop that passes through the middle of some squares, using only horizontal and vertical lines. The loop can enter each square only once, and so cannot touch or cross over itself at any point.

Numbers in the grid reveal the number of touching squares that the loop enters, including diagonally touching squares.

				5			
		8				7	
					5		
			7		5		
5							
	7				6		
							2

Hints and Tips

Routines

» Routines can play a vital role in managing your life, and helping you to fulfil your priorities. However, taking them to the extreme and converting your whole life into one giant routine is likely to be a bad idea, since it doesn't leave much space for new experiences or their accompanying mental growth.

» How fixed is your routine? Are you the sort of person who has no routine and simply hopes for the best every day? Or is your life a robotic series of duties and tasks? It is, of course, best to aim for somewhere in between the two extremes.

» Having a routine is important for meeting deadlines and for allocating time to things that you enjoy and satisfy you. However, you should allow space in your routine for spontaneity, so life doesn't become too dull or predictable. Dull and predictable are the enemies of brain training, since your brain is no longer learning as much as it could be. If you find yourself going through your days on autopilot, look for ways to freshen things up. The chances are that if you are not having to consciously think about a task, you aren't learning very much any more.

» To spice up your routine, you could even just try changing the order in which you do things, although changing the tasks themselves is even better. These can be simple changes, such as getting a drink from a different place, taking a new route to work, or trying a different class at the gym – anything that disrupts your usual routine is worth a go. Familiarity is great for comfort, but you don't want to get stuck doing the same thing every day. The little changes you make to your life can have a big impact on your mental health.

Creative Pixels

The empty boxes below are just waiting to be filled in – but what should go in them? Well, that's up to you. You could shade them to make some "pixel art". You could create perhaps an arcade ghost, or a smiley face, or maybe a flower. Or perhaps you should write letters in some of the boxes. You could even shade them at random, or in a pattern, and see what results. It's entirely up to you. There is no "right" or "wrong" answer to this puzzle.

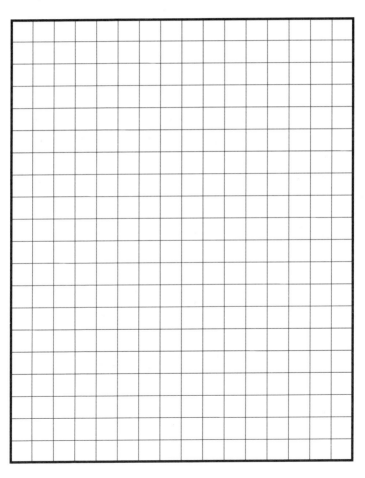

Lighthouses

Place ships in some of the grid squares, so that every ship is lit by at least one lighthouse. Lighthouses are the numbered, black squares. Lighthouses illuminate all squares in the same row or column, irrespective of whether another ship or lighthouse is in the way.

Each lighthouse must light up the given number of ships. Also, ships cannot touch either each other or a lighthouse – not even diagonally.

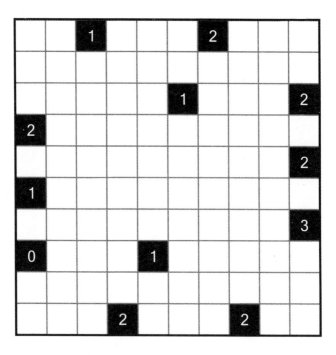

Easy as A, B, C

Place the letters A, B and C once each into every row and column of the grid. This means that two squares in each row and column will remain empty.

Letters given outside the grid reveal the letter that is encountered first when reading along that row or column from the given letter.

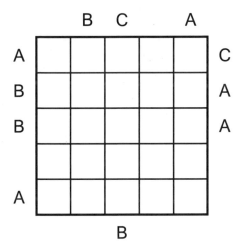

Light Up

Draw light bulbs in some of the squares so that every white square is lit. Light bulbs illuminate all squares in the same row or column until the first black square they encounter – i.e. light does not pass through the black squares. Light bulbs cannot illuminate one another, although more than one light bulb may illuminate an empty square.

Squares with numbers must contain that many light bulbs in the adjacent squares (i.e. squares touching to the left, right, above or below). Not all light bulbs are necessarily indicated by number clues, however.

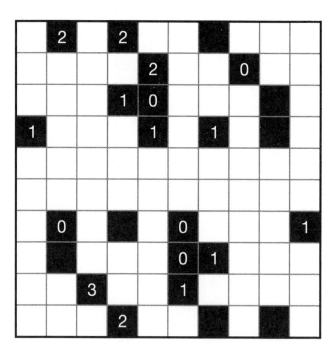

LITS

Shade some squares to create one tetromino within each bold-lined area. A tetromino is a shape made up of four adjacently touching squares. Tetrominoes must be L, I, T or S shapes, but not a solid 2×2 box, so these are the four options:

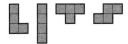

All shaded squares in the puzzle must form a single connected area, as in the example solution to the right. Conversely, there must not be any shaded areas of 2×2 squares (or larger).

No two of the same type of tetromino (L, I, T or S) may touch, except diagonally. Reflections and rotations of the same type of tetromino still count as the same tetromino, and therefore may not touch one another.

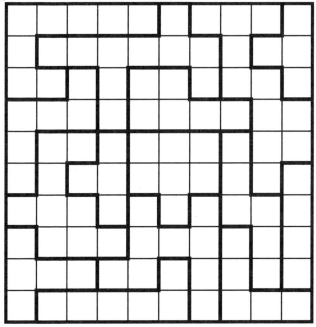

Killer Sudoku

Place a digit from 1 to 9 into every square so that each digit appears once in every row, column and bold-lined 3×3 box.

Digits in each dashed-line cage must add together to give the total printed at the top-left of that dashed-line cage. Digits cannot be repeated within any individual dashed-line cage.

Link Words

Each of the following pairs of words secretly conceals a third word. This third word can be added to the end of the first word, and the start of the second word, to form two new words.

Can you reveal all six hidden words? For example, GRID _____ SMITH would be hiding the word LOCK, to make GRIDLOCK and LOCKSMITH.

CAN _ _ _ ICE

MAR _ _ _ TING

REAP _ _ _ _ LED

DIS _ _ _ _ _ WORK

BUTTER _ _ _ OVER

Masyu

Draw a single loop that travels through the middle of some squares, using only horizontal and vertical lines. The loop must visit all of the circles.

The loop must make a 90-degree turn in all squares with a shaded circle, and then pass straight through the next square on both sides of the turn (i.e. may not turn in the immediately following or preceding square). Conversely, the loop must pass straight through a white circle without turning, but it must turn in at least one of the preceding or following squares.

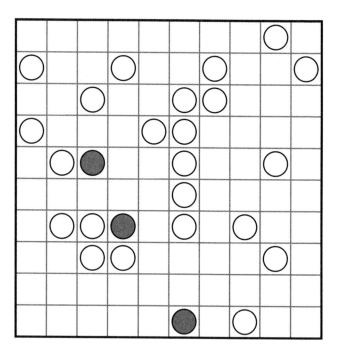

Brain Chains

Mental arithmetic skills are incredibly important in everyday life, whether you're making sure you aren't being overcharged when shopping, or working out what to pay when you have to split a restaurant bill. For practice, try solving all of these brain chain puzzles without making any written notes – that is, just in your head. For each chain, follow every step in turn from the given number until you reach the final result. Write this number in the box at the end of the chain.

| **36** | -25% | -11 | +25 | -31 | ×1/2 | RESULT |

| **6** | +1 | ×3 | +45 | ÷6 | ×4 | RESULT |

| **18** | ×1/2 | ÷3 | +51 | +50% | -25 | RESULT |

| **27** | ÷3 | √ | ×13 | +40 | -39 | RESULT |

| **17** | ×13 | -144 | +38 | -88 | +86 | RESULT |

Number Wall

Test your number skills by writing a number from 0 to 9 into every empty square of this numerical wall.

Numbers must be placed so that each column of white squares adds up to the value given in the bottom, shaded square of that column. For example, the five white squares in the first column must sum to a total of 20.

Identical numbers cannot touch – not even diagonally.

Finally, a number cannot repeat within a single row. This means that every row must contain each number from 0 to 9 exactly once each. Note that numbers *can* repeat within a column, subject to the no-touching rule.

		2			9	7			0
			3				0	7	
2			8		3	6			
	0			2		7			
			1	9	0	8	3	6	4
20	20	21	16	31	21	30	16	31	19

Rectangles

Draw along some of the dashed lines to divide the grid up into a set of squares and rectangles, so that every shape contains exactly one number. The printed number contained within each shape must be exactly equal to the number of grid squares within that shape.

All grid squares must belong to exactly one square or one rectangle.

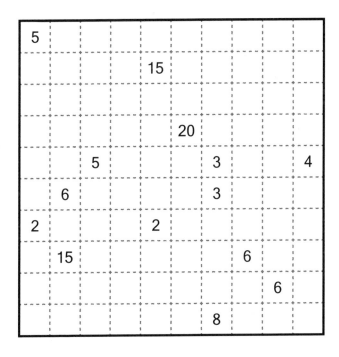

Hints and Tips

On the Tip of Your Tongue

» How often have you struggled to remember a word? It can feel like it's right on the tip of your tongue – and yet you can't quite retrieve it – until you do, sometimes far too late! It is normal in these cases to be fairly sure that you remember the first letter of the word, but not the rest. This is a common experience, since it turns out that the first letter is really important to help us identify the rest of the word, and our brains seem to index words by their first letters. Sometimes the memory retrieval gets stuck at an intermediate step – your brain goes to retrieve the word from the right part of your memory, using its initial letter, but is unable to find the actual full word.

» The connection between comprehending a word and its first letter is so strong that even when the letters of a word are jumbled up it can usually still be read, so long as the last letter is still in the right place too. For example, yuo sohlud be albe to raed tihs – you should be able to read this.

» A corollary of the tip of the tongue effect is that anagrams – or any puzzle with a jumble of the letters within a word – are much easier to solve when we know the first letter. This also helps explain why, in a crossword, it is much more useful to know the first letter of a word than any of the other letters – often sometimes still more helpful than knowing even multiple other letters of the word.

Futoshiki

Place a digit from 1 to 7 into each empty square, so that each digit appears once in every row and column. You must place the numbers so they obey the inequality signs between some squares. The arrow always points to the smaller of the two numbers.

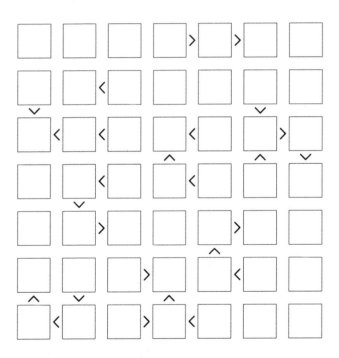

Nurikabe

Shade some of the empty squares so that each number remains in an unshaded region of the given number of squares. There must be exactly one number in each unshaded region in the completed puzzle.

Shaded squares cannot form any 2×2 (or larger) areas, and all shaded squares must also form a single continuous region.

Regions count as continuous if squares touch to the left, right, above or below – but not diagonally.

		2					4		
								3	
1						5			
2			4				1		
									4
		3							
2								1	
					5				

Solutions

1.

5 > 1	3	7	6	2 < 4

Row 1: 5 > 1 | 3 | 7 | 6 | 2 < 4
Row 2: 2 | 5 | 1 | 4 | 3 | 7 | 6
Row 3: 1 | 7 | 6 | 3 < 4 < 5 | 2
Row 4: 3 > 2 | 4 > 1 | 7 > 6 > 5
Row 5: 7 | 4 | 2 | 6 | 5 | 1 | 3
Row 6: 4 | 6 < 7 | 5 | 2 | 3 > 1
Row 7: 6 | 3 | 5 > 2 > 1 | 4 | 7

2.

0	0	1	0	0	1	1	0	1	1
0	0	1	0	1	1	0	1	0	1
1	1	0	1	0	0	1	0	1	0
0	0	1	0	1	1	0	0	1	1
0	0	1	1	0	0	1	1	0	1
1	1	0	0	1	1	0	0	1	0
1	1	0	1	0	0	1	1	0	0
0	0	1	1	0	0	1	0	1	1
1	1	0	0	1	1	0	1	0	0
1	1	0	1	1	0	0	1	0	0

3.

	B	A	C	
C		B	A		A
B	B	A			C	C
B		B	C		A	A
A	A	C		B	
		A	C	B	
	A	C		C	

4.

1	9	6	3	0	8	5	2	7	4
2	3	4	5	6	1	7	9	8	0
5	0	6	3	4	9	8	2	1	7
9	8	4	7	6	0	1	3	5	2
0	7	3	1	5	2	8	6	9	4
17	27	23	19	21	20	29	22	30	17

5.

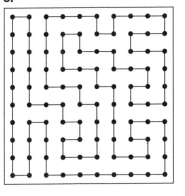

6.

4	1	3	6	2	5	7
1	7	2	5	4	3	6
6	2	5	7	3	1	4
7	3	4	2	1	6	5
5	4	7	3	6	2	1
3	5	6	1	7	4	2
2	6	1	4	5	7	3

Solutions

7.

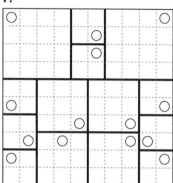

8.

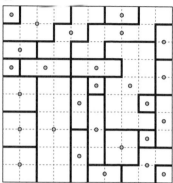

9.

| 13 | 52 | 73 | 58 | 29 | 8 |

| 9 | 72 | 73 | 41 | 57 | 30 |

| 17 | 18 | 9 | 3 | 24 | 36 |

| 38 | 19 | 90 | 18 | 54 | 6 |

| 57 | 19 | 152 | 71 | 143 | 110 |

10.

11.

- PAPER: SANDPAPER and PAPERWORK

- TABLE: REGRETTABLE and TABLESPOON

- REACT: OVERREACT and REACTION

- PHONE: HEADPHONE and PHONETICS

- TIP: FINGERTIP and TIPTOE

12.

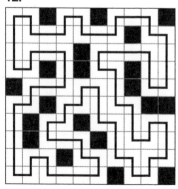

Solutions

13.

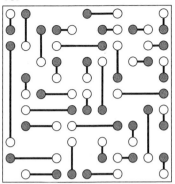

14.

- DOG
- GOLD
- LODGE
- LONGED
- LOUNGED
- BLUDGEON

15.

1	3	2	1	4	3	1	2
2	1	4	2	1	5	2	3
3	2	1	5	2	1	3	4
1	4	2	1	3	2	4	1
2	3	1	2	1	3	5	2
4	1	3	1	5	1	2	1
5	2	1	3	2	4	1	3
2	1	5	4	1	2	3	1

16.

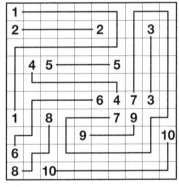

17.

1	8	3	5	6	2	9	4	7
5	7	4	9	1	8	6	3	2
9	6	2	3	7	4	8	1	5
6	3	8	1	9	7	5	2	4
2	1	7	4	8	5	3	9	6
4	9	5	6	2	3	1	7	8
3	5	9	2	4	6	7	8	1
7	4	6	8	3	1	2	5	9
8	2	1	7	5	9	4	6	3

18.

8	2	6	5	7	9	3	4	1
4	1	3	2	6	8	5	9	7
5	7	9	1	4	3	2	8	6
2	3	8	6	5	1	9	7	4
9	4	1	8	3	7	6	2	5
7	6	5	4	9	2	1	3	8
6	9	2	7	8	5	4	1	3
3	5	7	9	1	4	8	6	2
1	8	4	3	2	6	7	5	9

Solutions

19.

D	A	E	F	B	F	F	A
F	D	E	E	A	C	B	C
A	C	F	B	D	D	D	A
C	E	C	B	A	B	F	E
A	B	E	B	C	E	C	C
D	E	F	A	F	F	D	D
F	D	B	C	A	B	E	D
C	A	D	F	A	D	C	B
E	B	B	C	F	E	A	F

20.

S	F	L	U	N	W	E	R	O
E	U	W	R	O	L	S	F	N
R	O	N	E	S	F	L	W	U
W	L	O	F	R	S	N	U	E
F	E	S	N	L	U	R	O	W
N	R	U	W	E	O	F	L	S
L	S	R	O	U	E	W	N	F
U	N	F	S	W	R	O	E	L
O	W	E	L	F	N	U	S	R

21.

		530			
	268	262			
128	140	122			
57	71	69	53		
23	34	37	32	21	
6	17	17	20	12	9

22.

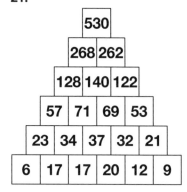

5	7	4	3	1	6 > 2
3	2	1	7	6 > 5 > 4
1	5 < 7	4	2	3	6
4	6	2 > 1	3	7	5
6 > 4 > 3	2	5	1	7
7	3	6 > 5	4 > 2 > 1
2 > 1 < 5	6 < 7	4	3

23.

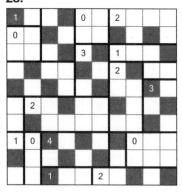

24.

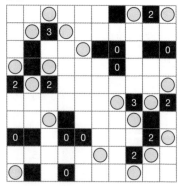

Solutions

25.

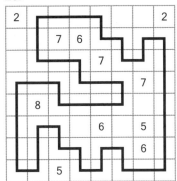

26.

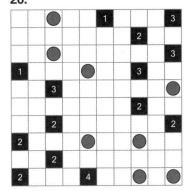

27.

28.

2	3	5	4	1	6						
6	5	1	2	3	4						
1	4	6	3	2	5						
5	6	2	1	4	3	5	6				
3	2	4	5	6	1	2	3				
4	1	3	6	5	2	4	1				
		5	4	1	6	3	2	4	5		
		1	3	2	4	6	5	1	3		
		6	2	3	5	1	4	6	2		
				5	1	2	6	3	4		
				4	3	5	1	2	6		
				6	2	4	3	5	1		

29.

30.

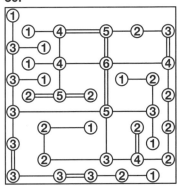

Solutions

31.

1 (4÷)	2 (4−)	6	4 (40×)	3 (90×)	5
4	6 (5−)	1	5	2	3
6 (12+)	4 (7+)	3	2	5 (0−)	1
5	1	2 (40×)	3 (2÷)	6	4
3 (90×)	5	4	6 (6÷)	1	2 (3÷)
2	3	5	1 (3−)	4	6

32.

4	6	5	8	1	9	7	2	0	3
0	3	1	7	2	4	6	8	5	9
4	9	2	8	6	3	5	7	1	0
6	1	0	3	7	2	9	4	8	5
0	2	9	8	1	6	5	7	3	4
14	21	17	34	17	24	32	28	17	21

33.

8	5	6	4	7	1	2	3
7	1	4	8	2	3	6	5
6	3	8	2	1	4	5	7
2	8	1	3	4	5	7	6
3	6	7	5	8	2	1	4
5	4	2	6	3	7	8	1
1	2	3	7	5	6	4	8
4	7	5	1	6	8	3	2

34.

		4			1		1
1				2			
	3		5				
4							2
							3
						1	
		2		3			0
		2		0			

35.

15	16	18	19	21	22	27	28
14	12	17	20	23	26	30	29
13	10	11	5	24	25	32	31
9	7	6	4	1	33	34	35
54	8	61	3	2	38	37	36
55	53	60	62	39	40	41	42
56	59	52	50	63	47	46	43
58	57	51	64	49	48	44	45

36.

	B	C	A	C	
B		C	A		A
A	B			C	
C	C	A			B	B
		B	C	A	
	C	A	B		B
	C	C	A	B	A

Solutions

37.

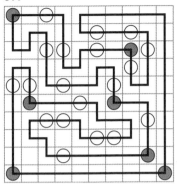

38.

O	O	X	O	X	O	X	O	O
O	O	X	X	X	O	X	X	X
X	X	O	X	O	O	X	O	O
O	O	O	X	O	O	O	X	O
X	X	O	O	X	X	X	O	X
O	O	O	X	O	O	X	O	O
X	O	X	O	X	X	O	X	X
X	O	X	X	O	X	O	X	O
O	X	X	O	O	O	X	O	X

39.

5	1	2	7	4	6	3
6	4	7	2	3	5	1
2	7	4	6	1	3	5
7	6	3	4	5	1	2
4	3	5	1	2	7	6
3	2	1	5	6	4	7
1	5	6	3	7	2	4

1247 — 2347
2467 — 4477
2677 — 1135
1267
1155
3567

40.

C	H	F	D	E	A	G	B
E	A	G	C	B	F	H	D
D	C	B	H	A	G	E	F
H	F	E	G	D	B	C	A
G	B	C	A	F	H	D	E
F	E	D	B	G	C	A	H
B	G	A	E	H	D	F	C
A	D	H	F	C	E	B	G

41.

F	D	G	A	E	B	C
B	C	E	F	A	G	D
C	B	A	E	F	D	G
A	F	D	G	C	E	B
E	G	C	D	B	F	A
G	E	B	C	D	A	F
D	A	F	B	G	C	E

42.

	18	11	16	14	16	15	16	14	15	
13	7	4	2	1	5	3	6	8	9	23
13	3	1	9	6	2	8	7	4	5	16
19	8	6	5	7	9	4	3	2	1	6
18	1	9	8	5	4	7	2	3	6	11
14	4	3	7	9	6	2	1	5	8	14
13	5	2	6	8	3	1	4	9	7	20
8	2	5	1	4	7	9	8	6	3	17
17	6	8	3	2	1	5	9	7	4	20
20	9	7	4	3	8	6	5	1	2	8
	17	20	8	9	16	20	22	14	9	

Solutions

43.

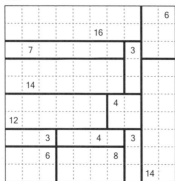

44.

E	A	C	N	U	I	T	D	O
I	D	T	A	E	O	N	U	C
N	O	U	T	C	D	E	A	I
T	U	D	C	I	E	O	N	A
C	E	I	O	A	N	U	T	D
O	N	A	U	D	T	C	I	E
U	C	O	D	N	A	I	E	T
A	I	N	E	T	C	D	O	U
D	T	E	I	O	U	A	C	N

45.

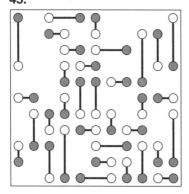

46.

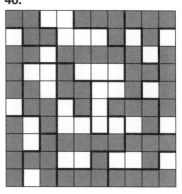

47.

2	7	3	9	1	5	8	4	6
8	6	1	2	4	7	5	9	3
5	4	9	8	6	3	2	1	7
7	1	2	5	9	8	6	3	4
9	3	4	7	2	6	1	8	5
6	5	8	1	3	4	9	7	2
1	9	6	3	7	2	4	5	8
4	8	7	6	5	1	3	2	9
3	2	5	4	8	9	7	6	1

48.

Solutions

49.

⌐12⌐ 6	⌐15⌐ 3	5	7	⌐28⌐ 1	4	⌐12⌐ 2	⌐17⌐ 9	8
2	4	⌐15⌐ 7	⌐10⌐ 5	9	8	3	6	⌐12⌐ 1
⌐6⌐ 1	⌐10⌐ 9	8	2	3	6	7	4	5
5	1	⌐6⌐ 2	4	⌐17⌐ 8	⌐12⌐ 3	⌐17⌐ 9	7	6
⌐13⌐ 7	6	⌐12⌐ 3	⌐7⌐ 1	2	9	⌐9⌐ 8	5	4
⌐21⌐ 4	⌐20⌐ 8	9	6	7	⌐6⌐ 5	1	⌐5⌐ 3	⌐11⌐ 2
8	5	⌐11⌐ 1	⌐29⌐ 3	⌐15⌐ 6	7	⌐9⌐ 4	2	9
9	7	6	8	4	2	5	⌐11⌐ 1	3
⌐5⌐ 3	2	4	9	5	⌐15⌐ 1	6	8	7

50.

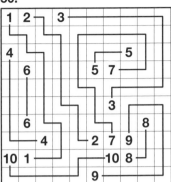

51.

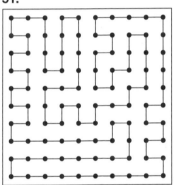

52.

0	0	1	0	1	1	0	1	0	1
0	1	0	0	1	0	1	0	1	1
1	0	1	1	0	1	0	1	0	0
0	0	1	0	0	1	1	0	1	1
0	1	0	0	1	0	1	1	0	1
1	0	1	1	0	1	0	0	1	0
1	1	0	1	0	0	1	0	1	0
0	0	1	0	1	1	0	1	0	1
1	1	0	1	1	0	0	1	0	0
1	1	0	1	0	0	1	0	1	0

53.

54.

D	F	B	G	C	A	E
C	B	A	D	E	F	G
E	A	F	B	D	G	C
F	G	E	A	B	C	D
A	E	C	F	G	D	B
B	D	G	C	A	E	F
G	C	D	E	F	B	A

Solutions

55.

56.

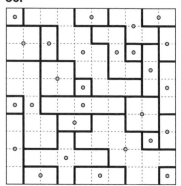

57.

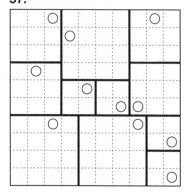

58.

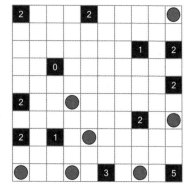

59.

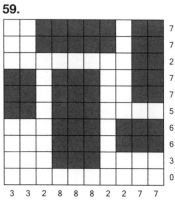

7
7
2
7
7
5
6
6
3
0

3 3 2 8 8 8 2 2 7 7

60.

4	3	1	2	6	5						
1	6	5	3	4	2						
2	5	6	4	1	3						
3	2	4	1	5	6	3	2				
6	4	3	5	2	1	4	6				
5	1	2	6	3	4	5	1				
		6	2	4	5	1	3	2	6		
		5	3	1	2	6	4	3	5		
		1	4	6	3	2	5	4	1		
				5	4	3	1	6	2		
				3	6	5	2	1	4		
				2	1	4	6	5	3		

Solutions

61.

62.

- BIG
- GIBE
- BEGIN
- BENIGN
- BENDING
- BLENDING

63.

- RAN: OUTRAN and RANSACK
- RID: PUTRID and RIDDANCE
- FISH: SWORDFISH and FISHTAIL
- WISE: CLOCKWISE and WISECRACK
- PART: COUNTERPART and PARTRIDGE

64.

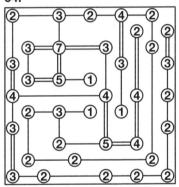

65.

4	7	1	6	2	5	8	3
7	2	3	8	1	6	5	4
6	5	2	3	4	1	7	8
1	6	8	2	7	4	3	5
2	1	5	4	3	8	6	7
8	4	7	5	6	3	2	1
5	3	6	1	8	7	4	2
3	8	4	7	5	2	1	6

66.

1	6	4	5	3	2
4	1	2	3	6	5
2	3	5	4	1	6
3	5	6	1	2	4
5	2	1	6	4	3
6	4	3	2	5	1

5	6	2	1	3	4
6	4	3	2	5	1
4	5	1	6	2	3
1	3	6	5	4	2
2	1	4	3	6	5
3	2	5	4	1	6

Solutions

67.

4	9	6	8	3	5	2	1	0	7
7	2	0	5	6	1	9	4	3	8
5	1	7	3	4	0	2	8	6	9
0	4	9	8	6	5	3	1	2	7
6	1	3	7	2	8	4	5	9	0
22	17	25	31	21	19	20	19	20	31

68.

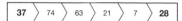

8 ⟩ 9 ⟩ 3 ⟩ 18 ⟩ 58 ⟩ **39**

37 ⟩ 74 ⟩ 63 ⟩ 21 ⟩ 7 ⟩ **28**

41 ⟩ 24 ⟩ 77 ⟩ 50 ⟩ 10 ⟩ **15**

33 ⟩ 67 ⟩ 46 ⟩ 23 ⟩ 15 ⟩ **21**

48 ⟩ 107 ⟩ 31 ⟩ 93 ⟩ 180 ⟩ **36**

69.

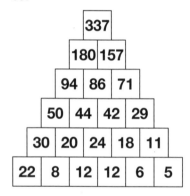

```
            337
         180   157
       94    86    71
     50   44   42   29
   30   20   24   18   11
 22    8   12   12    6    5
```

70.

C	G	F	E	A	D	B
D	A	G	F	B	E	C
B	C	D	G	E	F	A
E	B	C	A	D	G	F
G	D	B	C	F	A	E
F	E	A	D	C	B	G
A	F	E	B	G	C	D

71.

7	6	5	2	1	3	4
5	4	2	3	6	7	1
6	3	7	4	5	1	2
4	5	3	1	7	2	6
1	2	4	5	3	6	7
2	1	6	7	4	5	3
3	7	1	6	2	4	5

4567 — 1236 — 1567 — 1127 — 3357 — 1347 — 2345 — 1122 — 2445

72.

Only the shaded shape cannot make a cube:

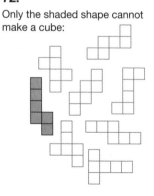

Solutions

73.

D	A	H	B	F	C	E	G
G	E	D	C	A	H	B	F
A	C	B	E	D	F	G	H
F	H	A	G	B	E	D	C
B	D	F	H	C	G	A	E
H	G	C	A	E	B	F	D
C	B	E	F	G	D	H	A
E	F	G	D	H	A	C	B

74.

$2÷$ 3	6	$6÷$ 1	$28×$ 2	7	$21+$ 5	4
$4+$ 1	3	6	$126×$ 7	2	$336×$ 4	5
$8×$ 2	$16+$ 5	4	6	3	1	7
4	1	$90×$ 3	5	6	7	$8+$ 2
$1470×$ 7	2	$1-$ 5	1	4	3	6
6	4	$1-$ 7	3	$6+$ 5	$3+$ 2	1
5	7	2	4	1	$2÷$ 6	3

75.

	24	6	15	19	12	14	20	9	16	
14	7	1	6	3	2	5	9	4	8	21
14	8	2	4	9	6	1	5	3	7	15
17	9	3	5	7	4	8	6	2	1	9
17	1	7	9	8	5	3	2	6	4	12
19	6	5	8	2	9	4	7	1	3	11
9	3	4	2	6	1	7	8	5	9	22
13	4	8	1	5	7	6	3	9	2	14
11	2	6	3	4	8	9	1	7	5	13
21	5	9	7	1	3	2	4	8	6	18
	11	23	11	10	18	17	8	24	13	

76.

3	6	2	1	5	4	7
5	2	6	3	1	7	4
6	5	3	7	4	2	1
2	3	5	4	7	1	6
4	1	7	5	3	6	2
1	7	4	6	2	5	3
7	4	1	2	6	3	5

77.

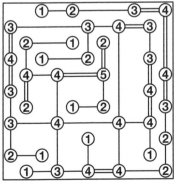

78.

8	1	5	4	2	7	3	6
7	8	3	2	1	6	5	4
6	5	4	7	3	2	8	1
2	7	8	6	4	5	1	3
3	6	2	1	7	8	4	5
1	3	6	8	5	4	7	2
4	2	1	5	8	3	6	7
5	4	7	3	6	1	2	8

Solutions

79.

6	2	1	7	4	9	8	5	3
5	3	9	8	6	2	1	7	4
7	8	4	3	5	1	6	9	2
4	6	2	9	7	3	5	1	8
8	1	7	5	2	6	3	4	9
9	5	3	1	8	4	2	6	7
1	4	5	2	3	7	9	8	6
3	9	6	4	1	8	7	2	5
2	7	8	6	9	5	4	3	1

80.

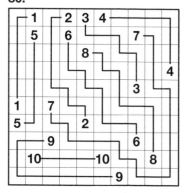

81.

2	4	8	5	1	9	3	7	6
5	7	1	6	2	3	8	9	4
3	9	6	8	7	4	2	5	1
6	1	2	9	4	8	7	3	5
7	3	9	2	6	5	1	4	8
8	5	4	7	3	1	6	2	9
4	8	3	1	9	7	5	6	2
9	2	5	3	8	6	4	1	7
1	6	7	4	5	2	9	8	3

82.

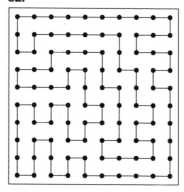

83.

10	9	8	57	55	54	50	51
11	6	7	56	58	49	53	52
12	5	46	44	48	59	63	61
13	4	45	47	43	64	60	62
3	14	37	40	41	42	26	24
2	15	36	38	39	27	23	25
1	16	35	20	33	22	28	30
17	18	19	34	21	32	31	29

84.

	A	B	B	
C	C	A	B		B
	A		C	B
		B	A	C	C
B	B	A	C		C
C	C	B		A
	C		C	A

Solutions

85.

86.

87.

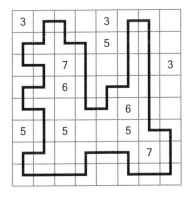

88.

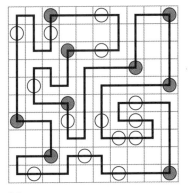

89.

			4			1	
	1						2
		5		0		0	
	4				2		2
1				2			
			4				
0			1			0	

90.

2	4	3	1	2	1	3	1
3	1	2	5	4	3	1	2
1	2	1	3	1	2	4	1
2	3	4	1	2	1	5	3
4	1	5	2	3	4	2	1
1	2	1	4	5	3	1	2
3	1	2	1	4	2	3	1
2	4	1	3	1	5	2	3

Solutions

91.

92.

3	1	2	5	6	4				
2	6	3	4	1	5				
5	4	6	1	2	3				
4	5	1	6	3	2	4	5		
1	2	5	3	4	6	1	2		
6	3	4	2	5	1	6	3		
		2	4	1	3	5	6	4	2
		6	5	2	4	3	1	5	6
		3	1	6	5	2	4	1	3
				4	6	1	3	2	5
				5	1	6	2	3	4
				3	2	4	5	6	1

93.

94.

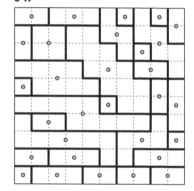

95.

D	G	H	B	F	C	A	E
F	C	E	A	D	H	G	B
B	A	G	H	C	F	E	D
C	H	F	E	G	D	B	A
G	D	B	C	A	E	H	F
E	F	A	D	H	B	C	G
A	B	C	F	E	G	D	H
H	E	D	G	B	A	F	C

96.

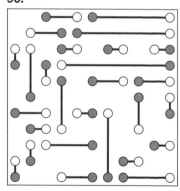

Solutions

97.

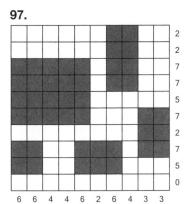

98.

B	B	D	E	C	E	A	F
D	A	E	F	D	F	B	C
E	E	C	C	A	D	A	D
F	A	F	C	F	A	C	B
B	D	B	B	A	C	F	A
A	D	C	D	E	F	E	B
F	C	B	A	D	E	B	D
E	B	F	C	D	D	E	C
A	E	F	C	A	B	F	E

99.

0	0	1	0	0	1	1	0	1	1
1	0	0	1	0	0	1	0	1	1
0	1	1	0	1	1	0	1	0	0
0	1	0	0	1	1	0	0	1	1
1	0	1	1	0	0	1	1	0	0
0	0	1	0	1	0	1	0	1	1
1	1	0	1	0	1	0	1	0	0
0	0	1	0	0	1	1	0	1	1
1	1	0	1	1	0	0	1	0	0
1	1	0	1	1	0	0	1	0	0

100.

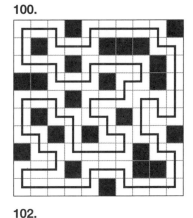

101.

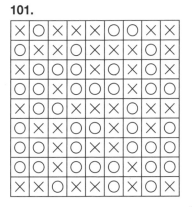

102.

Solutions

103.

6	1	2	4	3	5	7
7	6	1	3	5	2	4
5	3	7	1	4	6	2
3	4	6	2	1	7	5
1	7	4	5	2	3	6
2	5	3	6	7	4	1
4	2	5	7	6	1	3

104.

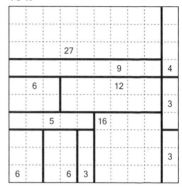

105.

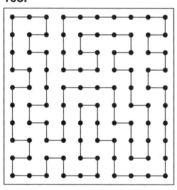

106.

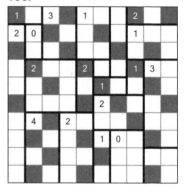

107.

7	8	9	3	11	1	15	14
6	5	4	10	2	12	13	16
39	41	37	35	32	33	17	18
40	38	42	36	34	31	27	19
45	43	47	58	30	28	26	20
44	46	59	48	57	29	25	21
63	64	60	56	49	50	24	22
62	61	55	54	53	52	51	23

108.

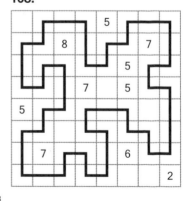

Solutions

109.

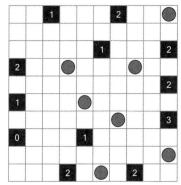

110.

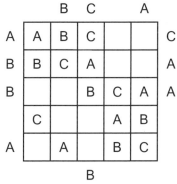

111.

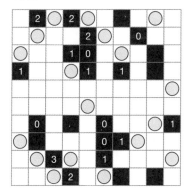

112.

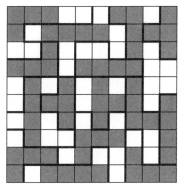

113.

7	3	4	2	1	6	8	5	9
2	9	5	8	7	3	1	6	4
1	6	8	9	4	5	3	7	2
8	2	6	1	5	4	9	3	7
5	7	1	3	2	9	4	8	6
9	4	3	7	6	8	5	2	1
6	5	9	4	8	2	7	1	3
4	1	2	5	3	7	6	9	8
3	8	7	6	9	1	2	4	5

114.

- NOT: CANNOT and NOTICE
- TIN: MARTIN and TINTING
- PEAR: REAPPEAR and PEARLED
- PATCH: DISPATCH and PATCHWORK
- FLY: BUTTERFLY and FLYOVER

Solutions

115.

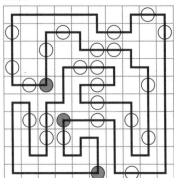

116.

36	27	16	41	10	5

6	7	21	66	11	44

18	9	3	54	81	56

27	9	3	39	79	40

17	221	77	115	27	113

117.

4	3	2	1	6	9	7	8	5	0
1	8	9	3	5	4	2	0	7	6
2	7	1	8	9	3	6	4	5	0
6	0	4	3	2	5	7	1	8	9
7	2	5	1	9	0	8	3	6	4
20	20	21	16	31	21	30	16	31	19

118.

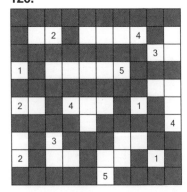

119.

4	1	2	7 >	6 >	3	5
7	2 <	3	6	1	5	4
5 <	6 <	7	1 <	2	4 >	3
3	5 <	6	2 <	4	7	1
6	4 >	1	5	3 >	2	7
1	7	4 >	3	5 <	6	2
2 <	3	5 >	4 <	7	1	6

120.

160